LIFE AFTER SUICIDE

Life After Suicide

The true life story of an artist that committed suicide by eating 12 ounces of rat poison, died, met the True and Living God and was restored to life on earth to tell the tale

Christopher King

Library of Congress Control Number:		2006910655
ISBN 10:	Hardcover	1-4257-4656-X
	Softcover	1-4257-4655-1
ISBN 13:	Hardcover	978-1-4257-4656-8
	Softcover	978-1-4257-4655-1

To order additional copies of this book, contact:
Xlibris Corporation
1-888-795-4274
www.Xlibris.com
Orders@Xlibris.com
33786

CONTENTS

Artist Chris King; The Mural Artist Chris King

My life as an artist began with a simple prayer at an early age. I often thought of that prayer and how insignificant it might be to the order of things but looking back I think that God may have found it very beautiful. I simply said one day that I would like to become a great artist and create because God creates. I want to be a great artist to understand God better. Through out the course of my artistic career I would tell that story to people in passing, as they would find me painting murals throughout the country.

The Crucifixion of Chris King

During my 18th and 19th year God called me into the courtyard of a church and asked me to take a friend of mine into the courtyard of the church. God asked me to raise my hands to him and in the next few moments God had placed me on the cross with Jesus himself. I felt pure living light and energy flowing through the center of my hands and through my feet. It felt as if I were in 2 places at once standing there and also standing inside the living heart of our Savior touching and feeling all his pain and agony . . . .

The Sinner Chris King

My life as a sinner began at birth although we never recognize this fact. If there was a prize for sinning I got the grand prize, first prize, second prize, third prize and runner up. I can confidently say I win and beat you all in this contest. What did I do? What didn't I do? In my life I was destined to murder my own children through abortion and murder myself through poisoning. The first child of mine died at the age of 18 or near there. It gets worse after this not better . . .

The Death of Chris King

I died taking poison. I took a total of 12 ounces of rat poison and a bottle of cold medicine the equivalent of Nyquil and a tube of insecticide. I took the first 3 ounces of poison and put it in a 20 ounce bottle then filled it with water turning the solid poison into a liquid. I was thinking at the time that if anyone should catch me they would not be able to get the liquid out of my system but solid poison could be taken out through vomiting. It took me almost 2 days to consume the poison. I didn't sleep for the entire event. Just to help things along I also found a tube of insecticide and decided to put that in my bottle of liquid solution just for the added extra comfort. I wanted it to be quick and painless . . . .

The Resurrection of Chris King

I decided to do the deed early. That was what I called it in my mind "the deed" I didn't expect to be returning and I certainly did not know what to expect. The first 3 ounces of poison killed me. My body became weak and started shaking with seizures. I lay there dieing slowly waiting for the end, my heart beat slowed to where I had to keep checking to see if it was still beating. I kept waiting for a massive heart attack or something. I could feel my brain starting to bleed. I felt the blood flowing inside my skull and in-between the 2 hemispheres of my brain. I also heard the voices speaking around me saying everything that was happening. The first 3 ounces killed me. I died and as I died I felt many strange things that are very hard to describe, most of all the sight of the true and living God. I died and felt my soul or spirit which ever you prefer leaving my body and as I left my body I felt no remorse over the loss of my body. It actually felt good to me to discard something so vile to me. I looked back and felt that death is not a bad thing but a relief from a painful life. I did not go to heaven or hell and I did not find my soul wandering the earth, I died and found myself in the arms and hands of the One True Living God. God allowed me to see Him, touch him, and be touched then God put me back in my body while healing what I had done to my body . . .

There is more to this story . . .

Suicide is a very serious subject. Our society considers this type of action to be taboo and the subject of suicide is not really confronted. We are simply told don't do it and the feelings and emotions and circumstances that surround suicide are never truly addressed and taken into a consideration that touches people on a personal level that they can relate with in order to help them. Suicide is something that we are confronted with and if we choose that path we walk it alone. Suicide and those feelings could last for months depending on the circumstances. You are not alone. This book does not condone suicide. I do not condone suicide. I simply try to write this book in the hope that it may help others by letting them know they are not alone and have had another person walk through this and lived to tell the tale and thus receive some type of sympathy as to their situation. You do not have or need to be alone when faced with the deepest darkest parts or yourself and the deepest darkest nightmares that occur in life. There is help. I found my help in Jesus. I found Jesus standing there in the middle of all my nightmares waiting to help me and then wanting to help all other people that go through this. I hope this book and its super natural story of God and love help you realize that we are forgiven. All our sins are forgiven, even the ones that we feel or think or are taught that are the worst sins to commit and can't be forgiven for doing. So what am I trying to tell you? Go ahead, commit suicide, find God and get sent back? No that is not what I am saying. I am saying that God and Jesus healed me and placed me back into this life to show you how far They are will to go with you in order to save you from eternal damnation. I was sent back into this life so that you may be prevented from going down that road of suicide and making that final choice before it is too late. Let Jesus guide your life; do not allow the circumstances that surround your life guide your life. Let Jesus take you away from making that choice. Let Jesus heal your relationships before they are beyond healing and too many hearts are broken. Get saved and stay saved. Don't just talk to Jesus, act and do what Jesus compels us to do. Read the bible, live the bible in your lives. Prevent suicide before it starts. My life is a testimonial to the true power of God and what God can do for us if worse comes to worse and we still believe. Let me help through my story if you are one of those millions of people out there either about to do this or if you are someone that thought about it real hard or if your relationship with anyone is in desperate need, don't do what I did. What I did can be easily prevented. Let Jesus into your heart in time to prevent these things. I made the mistake of doing this to myself. You don't need to be that person. Let Jesus help you by hearing about my story and what happened to me in order to prevent the tragedy from happening to you. Remember that not everyone that commits suicide gets sent back to tell the tale. This is a very rare gift that God has given me. Allow God to work in your life to prevent death and give you life. Get next to Gods Word. God is real. Jesus is real. It is all true. The bible is true. It is all true.

What exactly are we trying to discover here? Are we trying to figure out what I did? No, everyone lives and everyone dies. People commit suicide everyday. What we are trying to discover here is evidence of God almighty and son Jesus Christ. God is the great discovery that we search for. My resurrection is evidence of Gods existence and Gods will for us which is forgiveness under any circumstance even when we do what we think is the most horrible of actions. What evidence can I offer you? I can offer only this; God is real. The question now is what are you going to do with your life to get yourself right with God? Jesus is the only way back to God and heaven. Study the gospels and take these words to heart. Get hold of Jesus with all your heart and don't let go and don't let anyone take your love and faith in Jesus away from you. Lets look at this in a reverse angle, if we die and there is no spirit then God does not matter and salvation does not matter, but if God is real then Hell is real also and separation from God is real also, this means that spiritual choices need to be made in your life and once again the choice is up to you as to where you go and end up in eternity. God is eternal, where do you want to spend eternity?

This is not a book, as someone might understand a book having a beginning and an end, this is more like a conversation with someone about a subject and a topic that has no beginning and no end. The supernatural events continue to take place in my life and I understand things and what has happened to me less and less each day. This book or story is just a conversation with someone that has experienced a living mystery and that person, meaning myself, is trying to explain what happened as best I can, trying to explain something I do not understand to people that have never died.

IN REGARDS TO THE POLYGRAPH TEST

I went to the sheriff's office and talked with the officer in charge of the polygraph and he told me that the polygraph would yield a non-conclusive result since there is no threat of incarceration while I take the test. The polygraph is set to test heart rate and since there is no threat of me going to jail or anything of that nature the officer said that there would be no incentive to make my heart beat become excited.

Here are the questions that I would have been asked if the lie detector test had occurred. In retrospect, even if I did get to take the test people will still be skeptical and tell me I am a liar about many things. The fact is you will believe what you wish to believe when presented things in life. What I tell you in this story is true, it is your choice to accept it or deny it.

Questions for lie detector test:

Did God crucify you in a Church courtyard near the age of 18?
YES
Did you see a true healing in a girlfriend's hand around the age of 18?
YES
Did you take 12 ounces of rat poison and a 20-ounce bottle of poison?
YES
Did you die during the first 3ounces and then become immune to the last 9 ounces?
YES
Did you die?
YES
Did God refer to you as His son?
YES
Did God say to you "Christ has risen" when you asked him what would happen to you after you committed suicide?
YES
Did an angel speak to you at church and say these words to you "I will restore your family?"
YES
Has God been speaking to you for most of your life?
YES
Do you receive visions in dreams and then they come true?
YES
Did God anoint your head with what felt like oil while you spent the three days committing suicide?
YES
Did you see God when you died?
YES
Did you see God in a dream several months before suicide?
YES
Did God lead you to suicide?
YES
Did the devil try to stop you from committing suicide?
YES
Did you test the spirits when God began to ask you to commit suicide?
YES
Did you receive 100% of all signs asked for during the time you were led to commit suicide?
YES
Did God convict you of sin during the time of ra sha shana in October?
YES

CHAPTER 1

THE MURAL ARTIST CHRIS KING

What can I tell you about me? I once wanted to be an artist that made all artists tremble. I wanted to exceed my peers in everyway. I wanted to be an artist in a league all my own. I poured all the love and all the heart that I have into my work as a painter and muralist. I painted for days straight and it felt like I did not paint at all. I felt God himself watching me with pure love and pure pleasure in his heart for me. I painted for Gods viewing and Gods spirit of creation flowed through my hands and filled my heart. We created together. People responded with a great spectrum of voyeuristic amazement. Other artists loved and admired what I did and confessed to me that they did not even have the courage to paint something 2 or 3 feet wide. I was painting murals hundreds of feet long and dozens of feet tall. I poured my heart and soul and all of me into the things that I created. I tried to give and inspire people but people never saw the thing that I wanted to show people. This is the same conversation that I always have with people. It starts like this, "I wish that I had your talent . . ." That moment right there is the beginning of what I was trying to inspire in people. When people look at my talent and watch me paint, at some point in their mind they always imagine themselves with my ability. For a brief moment they imagine themselves with some ability larger than what they have. People imagine themselves as something more than they are. This is my hope for people, to become something more than they are inside and see themselves being added to from the inside out not being taken away from as evil brings destruction in our hearts.

Let me say this in another way. I don't want people to look at me and see what I can do, I want people to look at me and see what they can do if they decide to tap into their potential of creativity. Enjoy the murals shown here. It took me a lifetime of study and dedication to learn my craft. I learned my craft in the midst of all other chaos that was happening to me in this book. No matter what happened to me, I created, I painted.

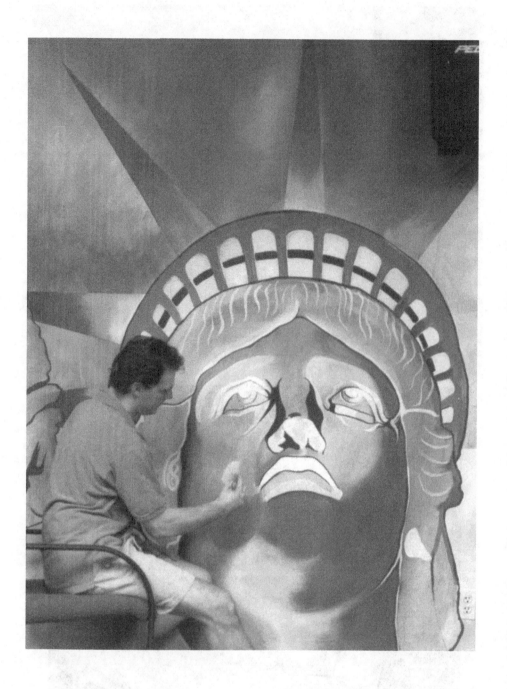

CHAPTER 2

THE CRUCIFIXION

**I open this chapter with an exert from The Gospel of Phillip . . .
The Eucharist is Jesus. For he is called in Syriac "Pharisatha," which
is "the one who is spread out," for Jesus came to crucify the world . . .**

The night in the courtyard . . .

What can I say about this night? I will not embellish or exaggerate. I will simply try and explain as simply as possible what has happened to me and then let you decide what this means to you and how it affects you. It is not given to me to be your judge or to choose for you what you believe and disbelieve. What is given to me is to simply be a viable witness for you as to what happened to me that night and be honest and plain about it. If I lie about what happened to me then I lie about God himself. No Child of God that is faithful will violate that ordnance but one and we try not to speak of him or what he does. It is forbidden for me to lie about what God has done for me or to me or with me and I will and I intend to be faithful to this to the best of my ability and memory.

It was near the end of October close to October 31. I was recently out of high school, close to 1986. I was living with a girlfriend from high school and things were not working out for us. She was doing things at that time that would cause her to spend three years of her life in prison. God had decided to come close to me at that time in my life and as I look back I can see that God was there to comfort me and help me through the pain of that relationship.

God has spoken to me all my life in many ways, in all ways. God spoke to me and said come to the church and bring the priest out into the courtyard in front of the church. I will leave the priest nameless to protect his identity and the identity of the church. I don't wish to implicate the church here. I implicate God himself and what God did to me. I found the priest and told him as God instructed me.

I remember specifically what God asked me to tell him. I said to him, "If I opened myself up and reveal myself to you would you accept me?" He said, "Yes," and we proceeded. He stood about 100 ft away from me across the courtyard and as I walked to the foot of the statue of Christ, God spoke to me again and said," Go to the base of the statue and raise your hands to me." I did as the voice instructed me to do without any idea of what was coming next. I walked blindly onto the cross with our savior Jesus Christ.

The next moment was indescribable to say the least. I raised my hands and called to my friend the priest and God himself took hold of me. In the next few moments my life stretched out and touched the eternal or the Eternal God stretched out and touched me. Something invisible literally grabbed my hands and something picked up my feet and placed my left foot to stand on top of my right foot. That which is invisible then took my hands and began to stretch them apart and away from my chest as if a man hand a rope around each hand and wanted to pull in opposite directions. Then the darkness fell over my consciousness and the nails went into my hands and feet. The sensation was not physical at all. It was spiritual. The nails that penetrated my hands could only be described as pure energy that lived. Living pure energy that was from the true and living God placed me on the cross with our Savior. The hold on my hands was so strong that it felt like they were about to pick me off the ground, literally. The nails pierced my hands and feet and that moment seemed to stretch out into eternity. I became Jesus. Jesus became me. For one moment we were one. That moment seemed to last for infinity. Then God decided to put me down. In that brief moment, the priest had simply strolled across the courtyard and held out his arms to me and grabbed me around the waist. He said to me, "Chris, come down from your cross," and I fell into his arms. God himself released me and I fell into his arms. I immediately asked him what he had seen and he said that he has seen or noticed nothing other than him and myself. I began to weep. God had done what God did and did not reveal himself to those around me. I fell to the ground at the bottom of the statue of Jesus and wept. The only question that entered my mind was why? Why God why? Why did you do this to me and show no one but me. This question haunted me for years and became the driving force behind my fall from grace. In that moment I was still within the realm of being faithful. I was to see 1 more healing before my fall from grace.

I once prayed for an atheist that was sick with something like strep throat. We worked together at a fast food restaurant and she came to work sick one day. I asked her if she believed in God and she emphatically said no. I told her that she was in for a very rude awakening and began to pray for her to be healed. I asked God if God would heal her and God said yes. I quietly walked up behind her and touched her and whispered be healed. She went home and came back the next day fine. I asked her what had happened and she said that she was sitting at home in a chair and then a strange feeling came over her and all of a sudden her sickness was gone as if it never had happened. I simply smiled and said thank you God and went about my way.

The first healing that I had ever seen occurred before my girlfriend went to jail and a few weeks before I was crucified. My girlfriend had hurt her hand with severe bruises at work. She smashed her hand and it bruised badly. She asked me if I would pray for her because I had prayed for her a few days before about an upset stomach and she said that she felt better after I touched her and prayed for her. I agreed and went to the church were I was to be crucified and knelt at the base of the statue and asked Jesus if he would heal her. What I was told was very astounding to me. I asked her if she would follow all the things that Jesus would ask of her and she said that she would. She was a smoker and Jesus asked me to ask her if she would stop smoking. God would not heal a body if the person would continue destroying that which God would heal. She agreed to stop smoking. Then Jesus said to me that salvation was more important than her hand being healed so Jesus asked me to ask her to accept him as her savior and she did, we spent some time praying about that as well. Next we were instructed to wrap her hand so that the bandages hid the wounds and we were asked to stay awake all night waiting for our healing to come. We agreed and stayed awake that night. That night consisted of a strange series of conversations. We spent time making love and loving each other. Then we spent time talking about if that is what God wanted us to do; have sex before marriage. Then we spent time talking about faith and for what reason God would heal her. We decided that there was only one reason that God heals and that reason is love. God loves us, love heals, and Gods love heals. We waited and waited and the morning crept in closer. It was around 4 in the morning when they started talking to me. A voice whispered behind me and said," Look, watch here hand now." I was about to speak up and tell her but decided to stay quiet and I simply watched. She sat there talking about what ever we were talking about and started to itch her hand. As she itched it she started to realize that it did not hurt anymore and then as it stopped hurting she decided to take off the bandage. While she took the bandage off a presence as quiet as snow falling came into the room through the back door. I felt a spirit come in the backdoor, it quietly revealed himself to me and I watched patiently. The spirit did not speak his name; this spirit prefers to let his actions speak for him.

She scratched at her hand and took off the bandage on her hand. A pale look came over her face as she realized what had happened and she began to uncontrollably weep. I tried to comfort her as best I could while she wept. I thanked Jesus for healing her and we fell asleep. Soon after this healing, weeks later, I was crucified and she went to prison. What does this mean? What does it say to you? How does this story affect your faith? I wish you could all see a miracle of this nature. The presence of Jesus is the most amazing thing to witness. Now I know you have many questions about these circumstances but remember whom we are dealing with and about whom we are discussing. This book is about God and what God does in our lives. Forget about my girlfriend and why she went to prison. Look at the facts; God healed her in spite of her future in prison or her current condition of life's circumstances. God is not faithful to us. God is no respecter of persons or life situations. God is faithful to God and the rules of conduct that he sets out for himself. God will not violate his own will for himself and this can be seen in these few miracles worked here.

She, meaning my girlfriend, was healed. If she was never going to keep any promise that she made to God that night she was still healed. For all I know she is somewhere drinking and smoking right now or she is part of a church somewhere helping others, who knows? She was healed in spite of the fact that she was about to betray me and emotionally cripple me. God healed her in spite of her sin. Sin is death. God gives love and life. Look at what happened to me and look within the circumstances of my life and heart and take this into consideration. I was born poor. I was born a second-class citizen with no hope of a prosperous future. I was a nobody that believed that God had forgotten me and would never come into my life as he had come into the lives of others. Society refers to me as someone that has fallen through the cracks of our society. Even though all these circumstances surrounding me are true, God still crucified me and resurrected me later. For years after that night I considered it a type of anniversary and on that special night I would take a long walk sometimes looking for the one that did that to me hoping to be reunited and hoping to learn more and be taught more about what it all meant. God and I quietly celebrated our anniversary of the great mystery that God had done in my life. It is still a mystery what God has done to me, even now after my death and resurrection. Even now, after all the things and miracles that I have witnessed God perform in my life, God is more a mystery now than God ever was before. What is in store for my future? Only God knows; I know that I do not.

The bottle of sleeping pills: My first conscious attempt at suicide

Soon after my crucifixion I still tried to stop my girlfriend from doing what she was doing. I new it was going to end in disaster for her but I could not get her to stop and prevent her from going to jail for three years. There was one night in particular

27

where I had simply had enough and decided to end it all right in front of here and I went to the store and bought a bottle of sleeping pills. I went to the house where she was staying and made sure that she got to see me take the entire bottle of pills. I poured them all into my hand and took them all as she watched through the window of the front door. The police came and escorted me away and soon after I found myself back at the foot of that statue of Jesus. I waited there. I was waiting for the pills to take effect and "kick in". A strange thing happened to me, even then that I never realized. I took an entire bottle of sleeping pills and I never even fell asleep that night. I never passed out or even got tired. I remember thinking distinctly to myself how I was cheated and must have bought a dud bottle of real weak pills that never even knocked me out. For weeks after that I contemplated suicide and planned it but never seemed to get around to it since my failed attempt with the bottle of pills. At that time it never occurred to me that God prevented those pills from taking effect on me although it seems obvious to me that God and Jesus intervened. God has been preventing me from dieing all my life, to serve what purpose I know not. I consider myself to be no one particularly special in the grand scheme of life on earth. I will never become anyone that alters life on earth in a positive direction although I always wanted to contribute to the greater good of mankind and contribute to God almighty. I always assumed that I would have these desires in my heart to contribute but never get the opportunity to contribute. Why has God been personally preventing my death for all these years? Why is God keeping this a mystery, even from me, the one he saves from death itself? God has ordained my death to be an "impossibility" until I serve some purpose that God would see fulfilled yet this purpose is unknown to me. God seems content to keep this mystery to himself for now. Who am I to go against God in this manner? I'm sure that when it comes time even these great mysteries will be shown to me. God has never denied me knowledge, knowledge has been delayed in being given to me until the proper time, the proper time is Gods timing, not my own. I look forward to these great mysteries getting solved.

So what happened to the girlfriend? I will not say what she went to jail for, her sins are forgiven. This book is about God and what God does for us, not the list of sins we commit against God. I will say that we never saw each other again to this day. She called me about a year and a half into her prison term and thanked me for trying to help her and keep her from her destruction. She thanked me for fighting with her to prevent her own destruction and said that she finally learned what I was trying to tell her while in jail. I suspect that she found her salvation during her time in jail. I hope she is doing well and is close to God in some way. I suspect God watches over her for me since God knows the truth about how I feel for her in my heart and how I completely loved her and probably still love her. I know God watches over her. I know I still love her.

**Random events of my prevented deaths in my life
from the far past to the most recent**

All of these things listed here occurred after the night I was crucified.

I took a bottle of sleeping pills that had no effect; I did not even fall asleep.

I was sick with some type of food poisoning in South America. I ate a few barnacles while in Peru for some reason. I got real sick but never died. I went to Peru for two months.

I hit a parked car with my motorcycle going 60 mph. I never even got a scratch or bruise. I was a motorcycle courier in DC at the time.

I feel asleep in Alaska in 30-degree weather with only the clothes on my back and no fire in a drizzling rain. The temperature was falling and I did not expect to wake up the next morning. When its 30 degrees in the daytime then the temperature falls even more when nighttime comes. I remember a deep warm sleep in that cold weather and woke up feeling great.

I once overdosed on drugs. I took every type of over the counter medication that says to not mix them together and mixed them together and then wound up in the hospital. I had a girlfriend who had a brother who liked to do drugs and I made him something special from over the counter medication. We spent all day making it and the rest of the day taking it. Actifed, Sudafed, caffeine, aspirin, Nyquil, cold medicine Tylenol and a few others at least a pack each was mixed together into a great big bowl and then formed them into a small ball the size of a golf ball. We put them in tea and drank the tea. Once again I never fell asleep. I was affected but never died or fell asleep.

The steering column broke in my truck. This means the steering wheel turned in circles but the tires did not turn left or right. It broke as I came to a stop. What a strange coincidence. If it had broken 2 minutes before that I would have been going 60 mph on the high way.

Last but not least, I took 12 ounces of rat poison, a bottle of Nyquil, and insecticide and then died and was brought back to life.

God wants me to stay here I believe. Why? I do not know yet. My death has been prevented more times than I'm aware of probably.

Chapter 3

20 YEARS OF SIN

A brief glimpse into Hell

Soon after my girlfriend went to jail . . .

I spent a long while; perhaps a year or two, trying to figure out why God did what God did to me that night with Jesus. I was obedient that night but knew nothing of Jesus and what his coming to this world of separation from God really meant. God had always used me to help others but seemed content to ignore me and simply gave me the bare minimum to get by. God spoke to me about everything but why he crucified me. After years of frustration and pain over what had happened I decided to simply give up. I gave up and decided to be me without God or thought of God. I turned to my Artwork once again. There was no one to talk to about this and no one to turn to and the one that did this offered no answers to the gapping hole in me so I decided to turn my heart away from God. The event of being crucified did not hurt. The night that I was crucified was the opposite of pain and the opposite of hell. It was pure heaven being united with our savior the way that we were united. The pain came from not knowing why and for what reason or purpose. There seemed to be a great gapping hole that was left in me from being crucified. The pain came when God stopped holding me and put me back into this world. Going to church became increasingly difficult. Turning my back on God was not a one-time event but a gradual process that took its toll daily and chipped away at me a little more each day. Biblically speaking, I began pitching my tent closer and closer to Sodom. The more I went to church the more I would focus on my one undying question of why and this caused a rift of abandonment between me and God. I went looking for answers to questions that only God himself could solve or reveal and God offered me the opposite of this. The question and the statement that kept coming to mind was simply the last few words that Jesus said, "Why have you forsaken me?". For years all I ever knew of Jesus was pain. Then came the conscious choice of turning away. At some point in my life between 22 and 30 I gave up and decided to turn my back to God and seek satisfaction from other things. I went in search of sin and all its pleasures. I deliberately went in search of the devil and what the devil had to offer. I was made a master of sin. The devil himself gave me all the lust that I could handle and then brought me a little bit more. It never seemed to last. The more I took in the more it felt like emptiness. The more sin I participated in, the more I became numb to all sensation. I had become immune and numb to my newfound drug of sinful satisfaction. All the money that I had received was never enough. All the sex and women of the world never seemed to fill the gapping hole that was left in me by sharing the cross of Jesus. The pain was not on the cross, the pain was being ignored or believing that I was ignored by God. If I could describe my sin all I could say was that I participated in each and every sin there is, twice and then a third time just to make sure. I ran with the devil on a daily basis and I was good at it. It was natural like breathing. It was effortless and meaningless. Sin is easy. Sin is fun for a season. Sooner or later someone always gets hurt and that someone was what seemed to be me. All my relationships had a common denominator that went like this, as soon as I honestly fell in love with whatever woman that I was involved with, in those next few moments just like clockwork, she would break up with me. During this time my art career flourished but there was a spiritual price being paid for that as well and even something as wonderful as my art was going to be tainted.

My art career seemed to take off but it also seemed to have a glass ceiling. Nothing ever turned out right or as expected. The larger my contracts became the emptier things became.

Eventually things became so bad that I started turning back to my long lost search for answers. Some how the idea of true love got back into my head and I started looking for true love. The emptier the contracts became the more I became adamant about the idea of true love. I had still given up on the answer of the crucifixion and simply decided that this was a burden that I would carry around until I died and went before God to have God show and explain what and why this was done to me. I was on a new quest and the quest was for true love in the heart of a woman.

I searched high and low and the hearts of every woman that I knew and they all had the same answer. I was great for a playmate but something real was out of the question. A true committed relationship was not to be found. Could I find a married woman to fool around with me? Yes. Could I get several women in the bed with me at once? Yes. Could I have any type of sin in a relationship with a woman? Yes. Could I get a woman to honestly and freely to commit to me? No way in hell, literally. My reputation as everyone's fun time playmate had preceded me all over the county and women simply would not make any type of honest commitment to me. During this time I began my first time of real repentance although no one but me knew of my honesty and sincerity of wanting a real relationship.

Then one day I met my wife. My future was to be forever changed. All I ever wanted was to simply be able to do what I love, my art, and provide for those that I love, my wife and child. I received the exact opposite of what I had hoped for. Now as you read into this chapter of my life there are hundreds of questions of details as to the who, the what, the where, the when and the why. This book is not about me. This book is not about my list of sin. This book is about God and how God affected my life at this point in time. At this point in my life I turned my back to God and to Gods will for me so this time of sin is what I received. I was looking for true love but I was still not looking for God again. I was looking for true love in a relationship with a woman without God involved. This always ends in disaster. Looking for God was to come later.

CHAPTER 4

MY HEART BEFORE DYING
60 PAGES OF SUICIDE NOTES

From the Gospel of Mark16: 17-18
And these signs shall accompany those who have believed:
In My name they will cast out demons, they will speak with new
tongues; they will pick up serpents, and if they drink any deadly
poison, it shall not hurt them; they will lay hands on the sick,
and they will recover.

I always suspected in my heart that I would die over a woman.
I never thought that it would be in the manner of me killing myself.
I always thought that some crazed husband would find me
with his wife and kill me or something cliché like that.
Please God; at least prevent my life from being cliché.

It never occurred to me that I would die by my own hands. I will say this in the beginning before I write this chapter. I did not die of poison. I died of a broken heart. I did not die with vengeance in my heart. I died because all of those that I love were taken from me. I withered away and did not want to live because all those that I loved were removed from my sight and presence, this is why I died. Poison was simply an end to a means.

I will also say this. My wife is forgiven. I will not list her sins or try to explain all the pain that she caused me. That pain is indescribable. If you have gone through this then you know and I don't need to describe it, you already know. If you do not know this pain then I will simply pray to God that you never know this pain. I beg God to help prevent this wherever possible for all people. After dieing and knowing what I know about death, I consider death itself to be a joke. Death is an illusion of fear that is used against you to prevent you from giving faith to God so that God may move in your life and satisfy your faith and give you what you need. However, pain is no joke. Pain is eternal and can be eternal when one is removed from God and Gods presence. Death is a joke and temporary, pain is no joke and nothing to be toyed with. Spiritual pain can be everlasting. Seek salvation through Jesus to prevent this.

My suicide started with a dream and a vision. I dreamt of my son's death. I saw my son's death. Later in this chapter I will detail the dream that I had but for now I will simply tell the history and the time line of what happened.

To put it as simple as possible, my wife left me and took my son. I decided that I had had enough of this world and all the people within it. I decided that I had enough of sin and this entire world. True love cannot flourish in a world where a Demon and a Devil exists that constantly destroys the possibility of true love growing and flourishing. I had enough of this world. This world is the devils play ground and I am the smallest child in the schoolyard. We exist on a spiritual battlefield without any ability to defend ourselves. We are dependant on God for all our defenses; we have no real ability to defend ourselves without God. I had enough of sin and decided to end it all and leave this world to be with my son in the next life. I spent a great deal of time planning and waiting for the right moment.

Then God began to convict me of my sins. God began speaking to me again and started asking me all the painful questions that convicted me of many, many sins. God said to me this "You gave your wife a great deal of pain, what will you do about this?" I said to God," If that tiny beautiful woman can take all the pain that I gave her then so will I. If she can take the pain, then so can I . . . Give me all the pain that I gave her God." In that moment God began to give me all her pain and held nothing back. Once again I was back on that cross. Once again I was in two places, no three places at once. I was myself inside all my pain. I was inside Jesus suffering as he suffered or to be more precise, I was causing Jesus to suffer for me since Jesus is the Sinless One. I was inside my wife, touching and feeling all her pain that I caused through my sins against God. Now as I describe this, I can't imagine what it is like to be an onlooker. I can say for certain that all will come to know Jesus in this manner.

I can say this and what I say is a true sign that God led me to my death: In the middle of all this pain, the pain of me, the pain of my wife, the pain of my son, the pain of Jesus himself. God resides. God resides untouched and unscathed without blemish. God stands there inside all our communal pain waiting and willing to simply love us. God loves us beyond all that we can imagine God to be. You can never imagine God. You can only meet God and then you will know. God was waiting for me inside there and loved me and forgave me and led me to forgive my wife completely. God led me to forgive myself for all the pain that I caused others. God led me to repent of my sins against God. God is beyond any pain we can create or experience. With the slightest whisper God can wash it all away as if it never were there. God is all you will ever want or need. God is all that can satisfy you once you get to the center of what you truly are. You were created by God to only be satisfied by God. You will find all these statements through out the bible.

God had shown me the root of my sin and I began to repent. I was a disobedient servant of God and begged for my repentance in my heart. God placed me into her heart through the cross of our savior. I felt all of her pain as if it were my own. This pain was real. Jesus is real. As bad as the pain was I begged God for more pain because it was real. I suffered with my wife in a way that she is not yet aware of and will not be able to feel until she goes into the next life with God. God gave me all of her pain and let me experience it so that I may completely and fully repent in my heart. This is one of the great truths about the cross of our savior that we will all experience one day. On day we will all know each other's pain as if it were our own. This is done through Jesus.

As God supernaturally convicted me of my sins, I began to do strange things. I started calling people and apologizing for the things that they saw me do and the way that I acted. I repented in action as well as in heart. God granted me time to make amends in the here and now.

As all this occurred I systematically began to sell or give away all my belongings. I started writing letters to Jesus as if Jesus was real and I could mail them to Jesus. God led me to do this. God led me and showed me himself in a way that taught me that God is right here and right now with you every step of every day of your life and is not waiting for us on some distant shore in a far away land. God was with me and helped me through all my suffering. God led me to knowing how personal and completely integrated that God is willing to be within our lives. That time of my life was one of the closest conscious walks that I ever had with my savior. I hope we may walk closer than this with each other when we walk together one day in the service of others and not on the path of my own destruction. God taught me many things. Every word that falls from our lips is a prayer. Every word that falls from our lips invokes life or darkness. Every single thing we say and speak is considered a prayer and is taken seriously by God and the devil.

Then I put my property up for sale and went into town to write my last will and testament. I have a morbid sense of theatrics; inside I said to myself I should sign this in my own blood because of what I prepared myself to do. As I signed my last will and testament it felt like I was signing my own death warrant.

During one of my last visits to my real estate I spoke to God and asked God what was going to happen to me. I kept telling God my list of things that I did and asked if there was anything else God wanted me to do. I remember on sentence that still perplexes me, I am still waiting for the words of God to fulfill itself in time. I asked God what is going to happen to me after I do "the deed." God simply said these three words to me," Christ is risen." God referred to me as his son twice in my life and has referred to me once as Christ. However God has never referred to me as Jesus. This is very interesting to me. What does God have planned for me?

During this time my conversations with God were very in depth and I wrote about a lot of these things in my 60 pages of letters. I decided to test the spirits as the bible says although I felt it was just a formality, when God reveals himself to you, even when asking you and leading you to your own death, you know that it is God. Biblically speaking God has always asked certain people through out history to do things that were seemingly contradictory. God asked Abraham to kill his own son for God and many other things that we all read about but never understand. God asked his Prophet and King to kill every man woman and child and animal in a certain town. God asked Jesus to die.

I tested the spirits and every single sign that I asked for was given. One in particular comes to mind. I said God if you want me to do this and you want me dead then just let me get hit by a car. One night soon after that I was walking back to where I was staying and as I crossed the street something invisible grabbed me and slowed my step. A force that was other than myself grabbed me and forced me to a stop in that particular spot. In that moment a car comes around the corner and it was about to hit me. I could not move because something other than myself was holding me in place. As the car was about to hit me, whatever was holding me let me go, that which was invisible let me go, and I took one single step and the car missed me. As the car drove by there was a woman driving, how typical, and she simply and quietly apologized. She said out the window," I'm sorry," and drove on.

I can also say that when God decides to call you home, you feel it deep in your spirit. It is an indescribable feeling, there is nothing natural in our realm of physicality that can describe the supernatural whisper of God calling to you to come back to him and come back to heaven. I felt this for several days.

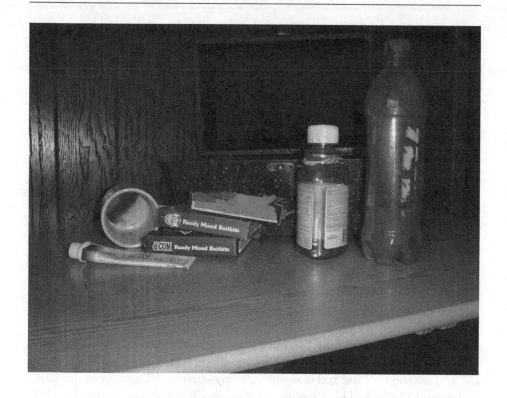

Three days of dying . . .

All things were in order and I was at peace with my life and ready to let go. I had gotten all my affairs in order, meaning property and all things owned. I auctioned off my stuff or gave it away to church or put it up for sale. All the money that I received I sent to my wife or gave to the family that took care of me. It was not much but I still gave it all to others.

God was speaking to me all through these times. One night in particular God asked me and expected me to keep my promise to him. A thunderstorm came up and lightning hit next to my camper truck as God spoke and asked me to keep my promise. Lightning struck so close to the camper that it shook my chest cavity the same way that a person feels when standing next to a very loud speaker. For a moment terror filled me and I actually thought that God was going to strike me dead with lightning. I reasserted my promise to God. I will keep my promise to you God. I went inside after that, waiting for the next morning and the lightning to be over. I checked the woods the next day to see if there was any sign of lightning hitting a tree or the ground and there was no evidence what so ever that lightning had hit the ground. Once again evidence eluded me.

A few days later near the end of October, I did "the deed." I went into my camper and started to take the poison. It was 4 boxes of mouse and rat poison. I took the first box and poured it into a 20-ounce bottle and then filled it with water. I let it liquefy so that if someone had found me they could not get the poison out of my system by making me throw up. This took several weeks to liquefy, remember I planned this for some time.

I started eating the poison by tiny handfuls at first wondering what was going to happen to me. I would put a handful in my mouth then take a drink of water and swallow like taking an aspirin. This takes some time; I did not eat it all at once but over 12 hours.

The first box of poison killed me. I sat there and slowly died. My body went numb and became very light to me. I never lost consciousness throughout the entire ordeal. The first three ounces killed me and as I lay there I could feel my brain starting to bleed. I felt the warm rush of blood flowing from my right hemisphere and flowing through the space between the two hemispheres of the brain. Blood ran in between the hemispheres of my brain. My brain bled and I could feel it. It was the strangest sensation. I knew I was terminal and it was just a matter of time. I lay there in the back of my camper, waiting for my heart to simply stop. I waited for a massive heart attack or something. There was no pain. At first I had seizures but there was no pain. The poison made my death painless. My heart simply stopped beating.

As I lay there I heard voices all around me speaking about what was happening to me. Then something strange happened to me. I began to call my own spirit forth and I called to me to come out of this body. I wanted to leave and never look back. I began to come out of my body and began to see myself from an external point of view. In that moment all the pain of this life was gone. I was simply myself, my true self, removed from the physical body. In that moment profound questions about this life were answered. There is existence after death. There is no death; only transition. Then more questions were to be answered. The one who created me appeared. God was there waiting for me, and caught me and held me. God held me and wrote onto my spirit. God spoke to me and whispered to me. God touched me and healed my body and placed my spirit back into the one place that I didn't want to go. I never even thought that I was going to hell or even considered going to hell, I didn't want to be put back here on earth. God put me back here. God is real. God is the God of the living, not the God of the dead. God gave me life and I am here to serve and live fore him now in his service. At this point I began to argue. I tried to deny it and told God something God does not accept. I told God no, against Gods will. There is no such thing as telling God the word no when God has something specific and particular in mind for you.

After being healed and put back into my body I proceeded to eat the remaining poison. I took out my bottle of liquid and started mixing it with grape juice. I took it a glass at a time in a coffee cup I had in the camper. I ran out of juice before I ran out of poison, there is still a bit of poison left in my 20-ounce bottle as a reminder of what I did. Then I broke open the other 2 boxes of poison and sat and ate until they were gone. I took handfuls of poison with bottled water to swallow. By this time another night and another day had passed and all my poison was gone. I had a bottle of cough medicine in the camper and decided to take it as a chaser for the poison. I also had a tube of insecticide that I put into the 20-ounce bottle just for some zest and kick. I was determined not to come back and have this be painless. God had other plans for me. When God makes a decision concerning something that God has created you to do, you do not tell God no. I was staying here if I like it or not, I was to remain on earth for a little while longer. As I look back even when I was at a clash of free will with God at this moment setting my will against what God had planned for me, God was still kind and loving but insistent upon me staying. God was not mean to me while I denied his plan for me; God still loved me. I just have to stay on earth whether I want to or not; there is no getting out of this for me. Why am I so lucky, Chris says sarcastically?

When I died my spirit passed through my body and my spirit passed through a bible that was lying on my chest. I lay down to die with prayers in my heart and a bible sitting on my chest simply waiting to die. My spirit came out of my body and found God waiting to catch me. I died in faith searching for God and Jesus. I died living out our savior's words of picking up your cross and following him even into death itself. I died in search of Jesus. When I died, I found them waiting. God did what I described here and so much more that is indescribable. As God put me back into my body Gods hand passed through the bible that was sitting on my chest. Later, after I told my wife this story, I gave her that bible. It is as rare as God himself. How Rare is God? There is only ONE TRUE GOD. There is no other.

I died after the first 3 ounces of poison and then took the remaining 9 ounces and was made immune to the effects. It was like eating candy or something other than poison. It was a truly surreal, taking poison and then having it take no effect, what a strange sensation. I kept eating it and eating it and it had no effect. It reminded me of the passage in the bible of taking poison and it will have no effect on them.

I took poison for two days and waited for it to take effect. It did. I died and was resurrected by the power of God and his son Jesus. During this time I felt and heard many strange things. As I lay there waiting to die I felt as if invisible oil was poured all over my head, starting with my forehead and then it ran all over my head. I heard God speaking to me about heaven itself and explain truths to me in a spiritual way.

God showed me a possible future for me. Tribulation is coming soon. A vision of my death was shown to me. I saw myself beheaded for my faith in God. Visions are so difficult to understand the meaning that we give them is a human meaning and God sees things through a divine perspective. I seldom understand what God says to me but that never stops God from speaking to me. I have always been grateful for Gods faithfulness to me. God is always faithful to those that God loves although we are never as faithful to God as we should be. What can I say about what I did? God showed me the truth about my sins and after seeing this and the distance that sin creates between us, I begged God for my own death. I begged God to kill me when I was shown the truth. The wages of sin is death. This must occur at some point in the life of every person here on earth. There are no sinners in heaven. There is no such thing as a person in heaven that is a backsliding Christian that needs to be forgiven. Death must occur because of sin. The Gift of Salvation through the cross of Jesus Christ is the gift of eternal life and the gift of the resurrection. I deserve death. We all deserve death. The gift from God is life. God did not let me read the bible. God let me live and breath the bible. This is how far I am willing to go with God and I am still willing to go even farther if God would only show me and direct me to what God wants me to do for Gods greater glory. So once again I make my statement: this book is not about what I did, I write this down, these events so you may see what God did and glorify Gods great love for us not my stupidity in my own actions.

My dream where I saw God . . .

As I look back, I have actually met or set my eyes on God twice. The first time was in a dream several months before I committed suicide. I was working one day and for some reason something happened inside me that made me say enough is enough. I had enough of the world and all the problems in it and all the sin in it and all the violence in it and something inside me broke open. I said to God," Enough is enough God From now on I will fight for you. I have been ignoring you for too long God from now on I am your warrior and I will fight for you!" I said this and meant it. All you need to do is watch the news for two weeks and you might feel the same way. Live in a major metropolis and you will feel this way at some point in your life. You might feel this way now and don't know what to do about it. All I can say is that if you are tired of the world then join me, fight for God don't just believe in God or have faith or be faithful, join me and fight for God to come here in this world here and now. Join me in my spiritual fight. The question is how do you fight for God, fight like Jesus. How does Jesus fight? Jesus beat back all of hell with the power of love, Gods love. All the hatred of Hell could not stand against the power of Gods love through Jesus. Jesus says love your enemies and bless those that curse you. Love those that can't love you back and forgive those that cant or won't forgive you. This is the beginning of learning how to fight like Jesus.

Back to my dream . . .

After making this statement of wanting to fight for God I simply fell to sleep thinking and expecting nothing to happen. God decided to visit me that night in my dream. That night I knew that this was no dream or anything from my imagination. I knew that it was God. I simply watched in awe. There is no way to describe in any language what you experience when setting your gaze upon the true and living God. You know who it is. There is no doubt. God started to take me out of my body that night in that dream. God pulled me free of the flesh and I felt myself being pulled toward him. God spoke to me even then, in that dream and wrote on my spirit. As God pulled me toward him my mind drifted. As I look back I think God may have taken me to heaven that night in my sleep. My thoughts strayed from God and my heart turned to my son and as I focused on him and though of him, I asked God, what about my son? God began to release me and slowly put me back into my body. I knew this dream was real but did not know at that time how it would fit into the events that would happen during my suicide. The dream was a foretelling of what was coming with my suicide although the though of suicide never occurred to me at that time in my life or the night of that dream.

60 pages of suicide notes:

In the following pages you will find my notes that I wrote down before dying. These are not normal or average suicide notes. When someone usually writes a suicide note they write it to other people. I wrote mine to God. These pages are each from a different day, I did not write down the date although looking at the envelope the date I mailed it was October 27th 2005.

Sometimes I would write 3 to 4 letters a day and sometimes only one page a day. I will transcribe a few letters here for you from my handwriting to the typed word. My letters always started out with a simple phrase, dearest God or Dearest Jesus . . .

Let me begin here as I look back on what I wrote before death . . .

I die of a broken heart never knowing or tasting true love. I lay down my life for God. I lay down my life for Jesus. The pain of sin my wife commits against me is more than I can bear. The pain of sin that I commit is too much for me to view. I lay down my life for my wife and my son so my sins may never touch them or taint them again. Perhaps one day within the Lords will she will see how much I truly loved her and my son. I lay down my life so my wife may never know fear of me again. I give my soul back to you Father in Heaven. My soul was never mine; it was always yours. The emptiness of never knowing real love on this earth and from those that claimed to love me leads me to believe only you, God and Jesus may satisfy my heart and fill the emptiness within.

In choosing between this world and what God is and offers, I choose the life that God would give me and not a life I would create for myself. I repent and rebel against this world. I turn my back on all the temptations of sin that are allowed to flourish here. I seek sin no more. I will participate in sin no more. I have been a horrific sinner my whole life. All I have ever known of God and Jesus is God and Jesus as adversaries not lovers. I lower my guard to you God and Christ and Spirit. I choose to fill my spirit and seek no more appetite of the body or of the flesh. This world in essence is temporary at best. I choose to go sooner than later. God calls me home. God is calling me home; I choose to follow.

I lay down my life for you, God our father and greatest advocate. My sins are now complete with beginning and end. I lay down my life for God now so that our father in heaven may see the truest fulfillment of my faith. I lay down my life and refuse to be blinded by original sin one day more than I must. Sin has kept me from becoming the true love I have for her and sin keeps her from seeing my truest deepest love for her.

I lay down my life for you Jesus and God and Father so I may receive and know the true love you have for me. I lay down my life so you may receive the love that has been placed in me for you. You have placed a great faith inside my heart that beckons me to lay down my life in this manner. In my time on earth I chased and cause sin to flourish and prosper. I turn my back to sin now and will allow the faith God has given me to prosper.

I follow God now into death itself. There is nothing here for me other than pain and torture. God has foreseen this in the path of life and has placed Jesus himself ahead of us to guide us into heaven itself.

God's kingdom on earth may no longer satisfy my heart. I must be with him now. I cannot watch over my son here on earth, the pain is too great for me. God has revealed and is revealing the true nature of sin to me and it is a horrific sight. I cannot keep my soul from screaming in agony as I look back on my life and all the ramifications that my actions involved. These past few months I have told others and still commit myself to the fact that I am living out a moment of conviction. God has been convicting me of all my sins and is leading me to willfully and knowingly put them down. It has been a living judgment. This judgment is often reserved for the after life but our father has decided to give this to me now while I live. My death is no coincidence. It is deliberate. My heart has often had a quit faith that no one has ever seen. I have often wanted and felt led to lay my life down for the lord. I cannot explain my relationship with God to you, it has been magical even in the most painful moments and times.

I regret never listening to that quiet voice that often said to me "Don't do that" and what I was told not to do, I did. I regret never answering Gods call. There have been times in my life when God himself was leading me to his side ad God himself asked me and beckoned me to pray to him and my response was "no, I will get there on my own with no help from you." I cannot imagine a greater sin in my life against God. I promise God, this will be over soon. I will sin no more against you and I feel and fear that I may need to lay down my life to do this.

I love my wife and son but I can go no further into this future. The pain of her absence is more than I can bear or ponder. I will follow the scripture, "til death do we part". My soul is too weak to ever allow me to even attempt to rebuild my life. I could not, even if I wanted to rebuild. I do not wish a half-life of convenient excuses so all sin can flourish and promises made are then to be broken. I want a whole life the way God intended us to be. I will keep my wedding vows and say simply until death do we part.

If you find yourself sitting there, asking yourself, "how can he do this?" My only response is this is an example of original sin. You can see your own pain but you are blind to the spiritual and emotional pains that were given to me. You see how you are hurt but never once considered how could I be hurting him. This is the sin I no longer wish to partake in. I refuse sin in all its forms in myself and in others. I go to my father in heaven for his loving discipline, teaching and restoration but most of all love. God's love is the only thing that can satisfy me now and has always been what my heart needed most. I go to find whatever family Gods will has for me. I go to find whatever wife there is that God has made for me. I go to God in search of my children. I will seek God now before I seek any person here on earth. I will seek God to receive the life that God wishes me to have. This world called the earth is a barren wasteland and I see God nowhere in sight. I go now in search of my true father and true love. I believe in the blood of the cross. God has made a way back to Him through Jesus. God altered himself for us; we are not altered for him.

God has not left me here on earth to be abandoned. God has given us the blood of Jesus so we may go home. The blood of Jesus cleanses us of all sin, not some sins, so within this statement you may find me forgiven. Another aspect to consider is my own testimony. I say God is calling me. God himself is calling me to lay down my life for him. How can sin exist in what I am doing if our true father in heaven leads me to lay down my life? I also believe that God is leading me to do this for my own benefit not for his. God knows me, although you all have been with me, God knows me; you did not know me. God calls me, my time here is over and I must go home. If God is truly calling me and I disobey the pain would be a living hell. I am being convicted of all sin through out my life and shown the errors in my ways. Once my conviction is over then it is time for me to go. I can delay no further in this world.

I have loved my wife and I love my wife and our son. I have sacrificed many things in our marriage and during our marriage that she will never see or know until our father reveals herself to her. I will make this final sacrifice of myself so that my sins may never touch her or visit her again. It is my wish that my sins never touch my son as well. When I am gone she will be free. I lay down my life for God and Son and Ghost for family and true love. Whatever remains of me after my life is washed away will live with our father in heaven.

My faith

God does not want us on this planet one day longer than we need to be here. Jesus was sent here to save us and rescue us, but from what? Did Jesus come so we can live long happy lives and work ourselves to death?

Jesus came so that the souls trapped in original sin could find their way back to God. As long as I could remember, I have looked at Christ and said; I would die for him. I have always looked at Jesus and said I will suffer for him as he suffered for me. I will share Christ's pain so I may understand our savior more.

The wages of sin is death. This is the eventual inevitable reality of our life. Death is a matter of time. Most live in fear of death begging for more time. God is calling me home. It is simply my time to die. I have had enough of how my family treated me and how I have been taught or led into every type of sin there is and still people think I should just stand here and be abused. All of the sins that have been inflicted upon me are all the sins I give back to the world.

The wages of sin is death. My deliberate death is my way of putting sin itself down to the eyes of God. I place my life down before you God. I apologize for 40 years of sin and self-mutilation of my soul and the souls of those around me. I apologize God for this sin filled life against you and your will for me. Accept my death as deliberate and with one purpose, I let this old life go to receive whatever your will is for me. Men run in fear of death. These men are probably men that have never known the lord. I have seen God and this action is what God calls me to do. My deliberate death is a way for me to give complete trust and faith in God and Jesus. I will trust and believe. My soul and this life was never mine to begin with; I simply give back to the earth what is the earths and give back to God what belongs to God. My life has always been one of opposites. As greatly as I have sinned will be as great as my faith and trust in God will be. It is just a matter of time. I am tired of all the pain imposed upon me by those claiming to love me. I am also tired of hurting others that I do love. We will all revisit these events again at the end of our lives and then if anyone even remembers me then your questions of "why did this happen?" will be known.

I reject and repent of this life and this world. I will follow Jesus and reject the rest. I follow God and rebel against this world and the lost sinful souls here. Before any of you rebuke me what I have done and offer some advice or halfhearted wisdom I ask you, "Are you God?" If you are not God then keep your opinions to yourselves. This is my time to live and walk in my personal faith and my personal trust in God. I will be disturbed by no other soul. I will see no other soul but that of Jesus and God themselves.

I go to God with my life to pay for sin. I go to Jesus to accept his blood of redemption and salvation and resurrection. I go to heaven in search of real family and true love. I go to war against sin for our father in heaven. My life will be the first casualty of the war I will wage on sin itself.

I would rather be in pain on the right side of God than stay here with all the fearful souls waiting for whatever. I have always fought against God my entire life. Now I will lay down my life to receive whatever waits. If God would allow me, I will fight as wholehearted for God as I once fought so whole-heartedly against God. It all begins with my death.

DEAR GOD,
DEAR FATHER, SON AND HOLY SPIRIT,

The wages of sin is death. I fall upon my own sword, the sword that I once fought you with; I now fall upon. I surrender to you in all things in everything. I have always placed myself before you; I now remove myself from this place of self-condemnation and self-exaltation. I humble myself to you. I lay this worthless life down saying I will never pick it up again. We both know how worthless this life is God but it is all I have to lay at your feet. I say to you I need this life no more; it is vain and ineffective. I place myself in your hands as you lead me to do so. I will have the life that your will and your love would give me and not this life that I created for myself. I hope you will find some favor in what I have done and will do.

Dear God,
Dearest Jesus,

I hear you across time and space itself. I come to you Jesus. I will make death itself a minor obstacle to see your face. The death of my life is a small price to pay in order to see your face. The death of my life is a small price to pay in order to be with you. I must know what I must know although it cannot be written here. I hear you calling me. I will come to you and deny all others of this world. I will hear and obey. I deny all other voices and save your own for my soul to hear. Our hearts speak together in a way that I did not know is possible. I hear you calling me and will deny you no more. Take me home.

Dearest Jesus,

I hear you calling me to forgiveness. I forgive all those throughout my life that have taken from me. I forgive all so I may receive your forgiving heart into mine. I forgive all who have sin for me, toward me and against me. To those that sin against me I now offer my life as well, for they take without giving. Now I give my life over so it may be taken away as well. What ever remains after my life on earth is over belongs to you Jesus. I gladly put this life down for you. I deliberately put this life down for you in a way that can only be expressed by faith in you.

Our hearts now express and speak in terms of faith and I believe the faith in my heart gives you pause to come and see. I wait for the moment that I hear you say to me; faith in you has made me whole again.

Dearest Jesus,

I see and feel you all around me now. I hear your quiet coaxing to come away and trust the faith that God has put in my heart. All roads lead to death. Death finds Jesus in the doorway. We are asked simply what do you believe? I believe in you Christ. I believe you are the Messiah. You are more things than can be named. I believe my sins are forgiven because you say so Jesus, not me. I believe Heaven and God and Father await my return. I believe because you say it is so Jesus, not me. I believe I must trust you because you ask me to trust you. There is only one soul worth trusting and that is you Jesus. You have shown me this in every single action and statement you have made when you walked the earth and when you speak to me now. Our time is now, this I proclaim because of the gift of choice and free will. I choose now lord, now is our time. I choose to believe you and drop this world and drop this life and drop all the false "everything" in myself and simply strip myself until there is only you and I that remain. This is the extent that I am willing to go; as far as you went for me is as far as I am willing to go for you. I know I will find you waiting for me. I beg you God never leave me on this earth again. I fear you may ask me to return in some way, I can see your eyes fixed on that fear inside me. My only fear is separation from you.

Dearest Jesus,

My faith in you cannot be expressed in simple words. My faith in you needs to live and breath. My faith in you needs to be lived and expressed. This time in my life is a chance to give you a gift from God you have seldom seen. Gods law and life is written on our hearts and not some tablets of stone or in a book. My life is a living expression of the will of God. My life has been a life of sin but is about to express itself according to Gods purpose and not my own. In your walk throughout time itself you have seen great faith in a variety of souls and marveled at their faith in you. Faith in you Jesus is a gift to you Jesus that is placed in the hearts of men by God for you to find Jesus as you travel. Our faith in you Jesus nurtures you and satisfies your soul in a way seldom known to all men. Soon the faith that God has placed in my heart will flourish. This faith in me is a gift of God to his son and I am simply a messenger or courier or better still a beast of burden that carries a simple gift from one soul to another. The only problem with this is me, Jesus. Will I release my faith and give it back to God and you or will

I crush it and deny it? I deny you no longer my lord and God. This faith that is breaking out of me is not for any man. It is for the eyes of God and Jesus alone. I will release this faith that is in me, to you lord Jesus. I must, I have no alternative and the truth is that I really want to do this for you. You know I will. My faith being released to you is a sign of the times. When all the world marches back into hell one soul will stand to feed you faith, that soul will be mine. I will stand and feed you faith lord Jesus. God has placed it in my heart and I must. I must because it is Gods purpose for me and for my very existence. I see you Jesus and all you explain to me and I hear although I am helpless to do anything about anything. All I can do is fulfill my simple purpose, which is to feed you Jesus faith itself as if faith were a food you can eat and drink. Faith is a fruit, which only comes from the human heart and human soul. Faith is what we all need and thrive on from each other. These signs of the times that you have shown me lord are horrors indeed. The world and all the sin in it are only counter balanced by your supreme grace and love. I do not know how to tell people what you show me and what is really going on in the world.

Dearest Jesus,

I see the signs of the times through your actions in my life and the state of the world. Hitler and all his satanic power cannot and did not destroy the world as effectively as the world left alone without the antichrist. An army arose to fight Hitler. Where is the army that fights to shut down the abortion clinic? Hitler should have kept his mouth shut and legalized everything as America does. America has become the very thing we wish to eradicate from the planet. An abortion clinic is wrapped in protection by the law. The law is wrapped in the Constitution, which is wrapped in a red white and blue flag, which is wrapped in a $100 dollar bill, which says, "In God we trust". The wrath of God will not hold itself back much longer. For every Jew and soldier that Hitler killed, I promise you that two dead babies from an abortion clinic will be put in the hands of the souls of those that Hitler killed. Abortion babies are stacking up in heaven like bricks in a huge building. Sin is so profound and prolific on earth that no one can see the problem with sin any more. No one even believes that sin exists anymore. This is only the beginning.

Dearest Jesus,

I cannot explain to you how horrific the world has become; all you need to do is see for yourself. You already know. Where can I begin to explain and where will it all end?

Nuclear waist created by electric companies is being dumped into the ocean by the gross ton so that a sin filled woman can us a toaster oven for twenty minutes.

Every law and belief that you have given to mankind has been broken. Everything that you Jesus and God hold pure and sacred is defiled and broken.

Knowledge is kept from those that need it. People murder people over simple arguments in the streets. People have lost all sense of self-control. The world is breaking down in a way that is so ungodly it cannot be described. It is the parable of the tower and the vineyard but this time no son is coming, God is coming.

I cannot describe in this short letter how bad the world is. I know that you know. When we meet I expect to discuss the state of things and whatever role that you intend for me to play in your return.

Dearest Jesus,

If my death were to mean anything, let it mean what our hearts and faith express it to mean. I only ask for one other thing. Let my death be the last death of the last true believer that existed. Let my death to you be so faithful to you in such a way that you must be compelled to return to earth by the sight of me. The scars on my soul will show you how the world is and the scars will show you what the world needs, Jesus. The world needs you Jesus, not me. God and you Jesus have given me such extraordinary gifts, I am the last of a kind of soul that only you can create. When I am fallen God I beg you to let me be the last of my kind to fall. I have often pointed at you Jesus and God in jest and said that one day God I would storm into heaven and grab you and bring you back here to the world. I would bring every living soul in heaven also, that is how much help this world needs. What I once said then in haste, I now say in earnest. Please return, you know the world needs you and is lost without you.

Dearest Jesus,

The world now is worse than the hell that you originally set people free from. The first hell was created by original sin. The new hell is worse than the first for the gifts and life and resurrection of the son of man are being denied here. Mankind is reconstructing hell itself on earth and cloaking it in fancy words and phrases. Men think they have the means to do and act. Men without God think they can build a paradise on earth. As we both know Jesus, a man the runs off to build something without you, runs to his doom.

Dearest Jesus,

I have often said this world is not good enough for my children. I broke this promise to myself and all my children suffer at the hands of their mothers. Now that my child has entered the world I am lost to him and he is lost to me. I say it is time. It is time to change the world itself for the love you have for a single father and one single son and one single mother. I claim now as your time on earth. I claim now as the time of your return. You know me Jesus above all others. You know I suffer our secret pain together. I say now is the time for your return.

Dearest Jesus,

I will read scripture and describe to you what it says to me. I will write this letter to you as if only you and I exist and this letter will reflect my personal faith in you and no other. "Except a man be born again, he cannot see the kingdom of God" John, chapter 3 Listening with my spirit and heart what do I hear? We are born into our earthly body, flesh and blood. We are souls in bodies filled and covered in original sin. We die at the end of our natural fleshly course of our lives. Jesus Christ came into this world to release us from captivity in original sin. Jesus has transformed death itself. Death has a new meaning with Jesus. As our body on earth dies our spirits are born again. Spirits that believe in Jesus live again through Him in His kingdom of Heaven.

I believe what I believe. This is what I believe. This is what your heart speaks to mine. You have in fact been misinterpreted all these years since you said this. I believe the ears of my spirit and heart and I pay the price with my life to find you and profess my faith to you. You know how blinding sin is. Could the whole world be wrong? I believe what I believe. I believe that I will die to find out and come to you for guidance and correction and the true meaning of what you said. You are the source of life that I seek.

As you walked the earth all who came to you asked of you something; you did not deny them whatever they asked.

John 6:verse 37 All the father giveth me shall come to me, and him that cometh to me, I will in no wise cast him out.

Jesus, you and I have seen many things. I believe in you so profoundly that I will not walk across water for you, I will walk through death itself for you. I believe that death is an insignificant thing.

1: It is inevitable. We cannot escape. Now is equal to later. The only difference is how long we languish in sin.

2: The only threat that death had was with original sin. When a soul died before your coming there were only 2 choices, the bosom of Abraham or Hell.

3: You came into this world. People who die now accepting you as being sent of God may be forgiven of sin and return to our father, Hell was evacuated of tortured souls and the bosom of Abraham was emptied as well.

4: After your coming into the world, death itself has no power over the souls on earth and is no barrier to any soul that believes in you. I believe in you and I believe you to be sent by God. Death has been rendered meaningless and no obstacle to a true believer. I am this true believer. I will lay down my life deliberately to show you what and how far my extent of faith in you and God is.

Dearest Jesus,

Once again I profess my faith. I speak to you of Luke 9: chapter 23

If any man will come after me let him deny himself and take up his cross daily and follow me. For whosoever will save his life will lose it, but whosoever will lose his life for my sake, the same shall save it.

As if only you and I exist, Jesus, I speak to you know. What are you saying to me? I will repeat it back to you. If I wish to follow you I must deny myself and follow you. If I am selfish and do only my own will and do not ever accept you as savior and never believe that you are Him which was sent by God to free me from the bondage of sin then my fate will be a mortal death followed by a slow spiritual death being a soul separated from God. However, if I lose my mortal life, deny myself, deny my own free will and give up this mortal life for your sake Jesus, accepting and believing all you say and do whole heartedly then I shall save my soul and spirit through you. Mortal death is unchangeable and inevitable, the only thing that changes are the terms under which I die. Will I chose to die and atheist or a true believer? I chose to do something so radical and believe in you in such a way that few have seldom seen. I chose to live and breathe your word and execute your commands with precision. I will not read of you in a book and wait fearfully to die. I will follow your word and live it out, as you followed the scriptures dictating the coming of the Messiah.

CHAPTER 5

CHRIST HAS RISEN

**From
The Gospel of Thomas
These are the hidden words that the living Jesus spoke.
And Didymos Judas Thomas wrote them down.
(01) And he said: "Whoever finds the meaning of these words will
not taste death."
1. And he said, "Whoever discovers the interpretation of these
sayings will not taste death."
(1) And he said, "Whoever finds the interpretation of these
sayings will not experience death."**

There are 3 different translations of the Gospel of Thomas so I thought that I would include all three here for your perusal.

All the poison was gone. It was now within my body, I ate all the poison that I had in the 4 boxes. The poison was in my body but I was made immune. I was healed and not dead. I had met God and been sent back. In that moment all my nightmares had come true. I did not want to be sent back hence the trip through suicide. I didn't die to be sent back but this is what happened. For the next few days when I went to the bathroom my solid waist was light blue, the color of the poison. It was solid poison. This was another strange experience to walk through.

I have been altered in so many ways. Death was very liberating when you go through death as a Christian and give all trust and faith to God. You can see my faith in the letters I wrote and you can see how God acted on my faith in the actions of God that I describe here.

The first person that I met from my family was my father and as I write this book he still does not know what has happened to me. I suspect that when the book comes out he will know by that time. As my father came to me and tried to see how I was, I was still defecating poison when going to the bathroom. It was surreal. Imagine talking to your father about suicide and promising not to do it then going to the bathroom and shit rat poison for three days. Strange does not describe this experience. IF God did not do this then who did? What am I to do now? I have no idea other than to tell others of God and how truly forgiving God is in all ways. I try to tell people but people don't seem to grasp how temporary this life is and how real Jesus is and how we will need him and the real value of the cross. You will never know the truth of the cross until God personally shows you the truth of the cross and what it means to your personal path of sin. You never realize the true value of forgiveness until God personally shows you all the things you did and must be forgiven for in your life.

The truth is that God is going to make you your own judge of your own life using Gods power to show you all the things that you did in sin against yourself and against God and Jesus. In that moment you will understand what it means to be a completely disobedient servant of God. In that moment you will beg for forgiveness. In that moment while begging for forgiveness you will understand the true value of Jesus on the cross because you will know all that you are forgiven for in your life. In that moment you will see how even before you were born God provided for your life in Jesus on the cross and then you will see how God completely loves you and loved you even when you did not know about love or even think of God. Does this make any sense to anybody? I hope so because your spiritual life and your eternity is dependant on this.

What will I do now? I chose to be the child of God that God wants me to be. I am becoming more and more dependant on God for everything and that is Ok with me because that is what I want. I will give my God and Savior everything that I have inside and then try and give a little bit more if I can. I live for God now and I live to please Jesus and I live to please the one that put me here in this life until it is my time to leave again whenever that is. I hope it is soon, but not too soon. I still have prayers that I wish to complete in this life. There are things that I want to do for God in the here and now that will be pleasing to God from the vantage point of eternity. I wish to leave spiritual value in places and moments in my life on earth that will be valuable to God and Jesus in a way that they value things, **not** as I might value something in my limited understanding.

Giving God something that God values is a hard task. For example, if you want to give God something, then commit murder. I want you to give a new value to the word murder and murder something completely different than what you as a human associate with the word murder. **I want you to murder the anger in your heart.** I want you to murder the hatred in your heart. I want you to murder the fear in your heart. I want you to murder your lack of trust in Jesus in your heart. I want you to murder the lack of love in your heart so that your heart may be filled with something of God in it. This is a thing that God may wish us to murder, not each other.

Chapter 6

Resurrection life

From
The Treatise on the Resurrection . . .
What, then, is the resurrection? It is always the disclosure of
those who have risen. For if you remember reading in the Gospel
that Elijah appeared and Moses with him; do not think the
resurrection is an illusion. It is no illusion, but it is truth! Indeed,
it is more fitting to say the world is an illusion, rather than the
resurrection, which has come into being through our Lord the
Savior, Jesus Christ . . . .

My new relationship with God, what is it? It is still being defined and explained to me in many ways through the word, through others and their interaction in my life. God speaks to me directly and reveals himself in many ways. I wait for a day of Pentecost as the disciples waited. Will this day come? When it does the world will know and see God in an amazing way.

Jesus spoke a few passages about what is being done to me. I quote Luke 20:34 "The children of this world marry, and are given in marriage: But they which shall be accounted worthy to obtain that world, and the resurrection from the dead neither marry nor are given in marriage: Neither can they die anymore: for they are equal unto the angels; and are the children of God, being the children of the resurrection. Now that the dead are raised, even Moses shewed at the bush, when he calleth the lord the God of Abraham and the God of Isaac and the God of Jacob. For he is not a God of the dead but of the living: for all live unto him."

Let me put into a few simple sentences what took me 20 to almost 30 years to live.

God crucified me and allowed me to join Jesus on the cross.
I became sin as Jesus did.
In my sin I died.
God healed me and gave me back a new life within him, living for him.
God resurrected me from death and placed me back into this world to serve God and others around me.
I live now with only one thing in mind that satisfies me, to serve and love God with all my heart and live and love for others.

God has forbidden me many things also

I may no longer play with life and death. It is neither mine to give or take.
I am forbidden to Judge others in any manner.
I am forbidden to tempt others away from God.
I am forbidden to lie about God and what God has done to me and with me, I must disclose all to everyone.

So the real question is this: Is it any better being here on earth now than the way I was then before death? Yes, it is the difference between life and death. I no longer fear death. There is no fear of death, only waiting for the next time of transition. Now here is the real question that I am confronted with: Is it any easier being this way, following Gods way to live? No, it is in fact harder. The responsibility to God is tremendous. God expects more from people that know more and God expects me to share and teach those that can't be taught or talked to about anything. It is difficult for people from heaven that live in heaven to come to earth or exist on earth; it simply hurts too much. Once you have seen God and touched God and been in any type of real contact with God and God ceases to be a character in a book and becomes a real being that interacts and touches and tastes and chastises your life and your being then Nothing and I mean Nothing of this world will satisfy or take the place of a single word from Gods loving lips. God's words that beat me are pure pleasure. The devils sin, that fakes pleasure, hurts me. Gods living words will show you and teach you the difference. God gives you an appetite for God and no one will satisfy this appetite but God. If God does not interact with you in this state of being while in a state of resurrection on earth in its present state without the second coming of Jesus then you start to starve for Gods word and a hole in the heart develops that only Gods living word from his living lips will fill. Reading the bible does not help, watching TV evangelism does not help, going to church does not help, the only thing that will fill the emptiness that is in us from a lack of God in our heart is the true and living God. Now don't misunderstand me. I love to go to church and listen to the TV and read the bible and I honestly can't get enough of it. I understand what is being said and it all makes sense now but even all these things are still of earth and from earth and still cant take the place of the true and living God and nothing can take the place of his interaction in your life. This is where the walk gets difficult and this is where people tend to fall away. There is a reason for that emptiness in you and that certain emptiness that we all share and all have and that certain emptiness that we all have needs to be filled. I can only say it as simply as I can and hope that it makes sense. I will say this one step at a time. We are created beings; we did not invent or create ourselves. I know because I met our creator. We are created beings, created by a being of pure living love. We are created to be in Gods holy image and that image is of holy love. We are created to be of holy love and be holy loved. We have an appetite for love and we also have a need to love others. Our need to love others is just as important or even more important than our need to receive love. Do you love to the fullest extent of your ability and are you being loved to the fullest depth and extent of your heart? If not then you will find emptiness in your life. This emptiness is a living thing as well. We are created for the purpose of loving each other with our hearts first and our bodies last. We are created to love others first and love our self last or even ignore ourselves and only focus on loving those around us. We are also created to love God and to be loved by God this is why nothing ever seems to fit in your heart. There is a hole that only God can fill and it was put there on purpose to simply bring you back to God to keep you searching for that one true being that put you here. There is a hole that only the compassion of others can fill, this is why we always lament and say those dread filled words; "no one cares." Lets list this in reverse. Love of money and love of all things of the earth and love of evil and love of hatred and love of self and love of the flesh can not satisfy your eternal spirit that was created from God and is a part of God that must one day return to God. You still think that you spirit is your own, and its not. You still think that your identity is your own and its not, its Gods. There is only one true spirit and that is Gods eternal spirit. God did not run down to the local jiffy mart store and pick up a box of spirits and put them in Adam and Eve, God pulled life and spirit from Gods own being. The state of being of Adam before the apple is Gods will for us, not the way we are now. This is why Jesus first bled in the garden at night and not on the cross. This is why Jesus was sweating blood in the garden and bled on the cross later. The first transgression against God and the place of disobedience from God was in the garden. God is poetic like that; I love it. We can't imagine Gods will for us because we can't imagine what Adams state of being was like in the garden. People still cant get over being naked in front of each other, no wonder people cant figure out Gods will for them and it seems so complicated. God is not complicated. Love is not complicated. Love is the simplest of things and the kindest of creatures and the gentlest state of being. I will tell you how hard it is for some of you to imagine the will of god for you in your life. Here is my challenge to you, try and imagine this before you even pretend that you know God. Try to imagine a world that has no money in it. Try to imagine the earth and all its countries and all the peoples and even yourself existing without money and existing without the need of money or the need to work for acquiring money. This is a difficult way to think of the world isn't it? No one can imagine their life without money or even what they will do to occupy their time. Now let me ask you a question that will help you put it all in perspective for you and I will quote Jesus Christ. "What father among you when his child asks for food will give his child a stone?" When you wake up in the morning and you fix breakfast and it is for a loved on, being a child, girlfriend, wife, husband, etc., when you fix this breakfast do you do this for love or for money? The world must throw down the crutch of money and pick up the true support in our hearts that is love for each other. Now you know how to imagine the world without money after reading this simple example. If we all unite to take care of each other then the world can do nothing but become a better place. WE all know how the world is though don't we? Who must we look to when the time for change must come? Should we expect God to do what we should be doing or should we be doing what we should be doing? God is coming back and the wrath of living love is a terrible thing for those that choose evil over good and hate over love. The truth is that it is difficult to be a person that loves in a room full of people that hate. It is difficult to get compassion from others in a world of self-serving self-centered people. The only thing we can do is turn to God and the bible for answers or simply continue to exist in a state of various shades of pain. You know who you are and what your pain is. You know who hurt you. The question is do you know how you hurt others? This pain of hurting others is much worse than that which was done to you. Only God can show you this. People are always willing to accuse others for what they did to them. Are you just as adamant to convict yourself as you do others? Do you have the courage to convict yourself of what you did to hurt other people or is this a big blank part of your life. Don't lie to yourself and think you did no wrong. The first thing that God does when bringing you back into Gods love is show you how you hurt other people, not what was done to you. Can you face this about yourself? This is the beginning of being resurrected into God. WE must admit the truth about ourselves in all its horrible forms. Then we understand the need and the real reason for Jesus and then we will sing his praises and be eternally grateful to God for the existence of Jesus and the salvation of Jesus. Until this day in your life Jesus is just another mystery. There is one true day that will be the first true and real day that you know Jesus and that day is the same day that all your sins are revealed to you by God and all your sins that you commit against God are known to you and all the pain that you caused and inflicted on others is known to you, that is the day that you will know and truly understand the mystery and need for what Jesus did on the cross. IF and I say a very big IF . . . If all your sins are not made known to you and all the pain that you have given others is still an unknown thing in your life then chances are that Jesus is still a mystery to you as well. There are 2 kinds of faith. There is blind faith that is simply trusting without knowing things and without knowledge and then there is the educated faith consisting of the 6 points of view of knowledge which is the Who, the What, the Where, the When, the Why and the How. When you know all these things then you have an educated faith that can't be stolen from you.

NOW IN THE TRUE LIVING LIFE AFTER THIS DEAD LIFE ON EARTH . . .

In the after life you will not be responsible for telling God and complaining to God and speaking harshly to God about what **others did to you,** you will be held responsible to what you did to others and what you did to your self and the sins you committed against God. God holds us responsible for our actions not for those who act around us. Now look at the world and how the world contradicts this statement. What do people do? All people do is accuse others and convict others but take no notice to their own behavior.

You can't lie to God in heaven. A lie does not even exist in heaven, a lie can't even exist within the immediate vicinity of God almighty; God does not allow this. You must understand that in the after life you do not ask God to forgive you for what others did to you; you ask God to forgive you for your sins against God and the pain you inflicted on others.

I will describe heaven from a negative point of view as it was described to me. Knowing heaven and understanding it starts with a lie. Imagine a lie. Imagine a lie in a person's heart. Look at a lie in your own heart. It has value and it occupies space in the spiritual realm. A lie in this world lives and breathes and spreads. We all know this and have seen this in ourselves and in the hearts of others. WE have the ability to live out a lie on a singular level and on a collective level and suffer from its consequences and feel its pain. Now imagine all these other things, doubt, fear, hate and all things evil or dark and sinister.

In Heaven a lie cannot exist. It is impossible for you to think, feel or even speak a lie; God will not allow it in his heart or in the heart of those around God. There is no presence of LIE in anyone in heaven; there is also no doubt, fear or hatred etc. This is the great separation of earth and heaven. We have free will and we chose to let lies grow. Now look in the hearts of those around you. Do you think that every one in your family can handle knowing everything there is to know about your life and not condemn you? People condemn each other from the point of view of the bystander on earth but it is not so in Heaven. In heaven they know everything there is to know about you. Your life is an open book for all to see and feel and touch and experience. In heaven no one condemns you. All hearts and spirits in heaven rejoice when a sinner comes to repentance and all hearts and spirits in heaven hope and expect us to be joining them in heaven. This is the life that is ahead of you. Heaven is waiting for you to join Heaven.

The sooner you get started doing these things that I explain here the sooner your life will be better not worse. Don't wait for God to adopt you as a son or daughter. Adopt the ways of heaven and help bring heaven to earth one human heart at a time. Help God resurrect you.

SPIRITUAL VALUE VS CARNAL VALUES

God has been teaching me values that are much different than those taught by people of this world or the natural tendencies of the carnal flesh and man without God.

IN HEAVEN THERE IS NO SUCH THING AS MONEY, THERE IS NO NEED FOR MONEY. WHAT DO THEY VALUE THERE?

God is pure living love. What does pure living love value? Living Love values acts of Living Love. A being made of pure living love such as God and Jesus value acts of love and expressions of love in their most selfless of expressions. How can God condone money when men kill each other over it? How can a man know the difference between that which is real and that which is false when that same man values an inanimate object such as money, (a piece of paper) over his life and the lives of those around him. Physical life is temporary at best. Physical form is in a constant state of decomposition. Physical life at its best is systematically problematic. If a man follows his own creation of philosophy then he is becoming the author of his own demise.

I am the author of my own corruption
My appetite is for self-destruction
My own worst enemy is sad to see
My own worst enemy can be only me

When I endeavor to go Gods way
My own thoughts ask me to stray
When I stay within God purpose
All I can do is serve others first

Flesh and Spirit are as different as night and day. They can never touch. Flesh is animated by spirit. When flesh dies the spirit is free. Flesh generates a false type of temporary love that confuses and confounds most relationships. God is pure and living love; they are one and the same not something created by the other. We create love and hate in our emotional physicality. God is true living love that does not quit or give up. So you must ask yourself, what does God value from the vantage point of heaven and what will we value when looking back from there to here. What will you look back upon in your life that you will consider to be selfless love and selfish actions? What spiritual currency is traded in heaven that inspires God to weep tears of joy for you? Have you ever even wanted to consider God weeping tears of joy over the beautiful things that you have done? God is a fierce lover. Hell is weak. Hate is weak. God's love triumphed over hell through Jesus on the cross. Hell and all hells hate did not win against Gods love. God's love is a fierce thing that is so gentle that the hardest of hearts break against it. What have you really done with your life other than waist it? What is the purpose of life? If it is a random series of events then it has no value. If life and this world are in fact created then it must have a value. The true value of life is known in detail to the one that created it; not to those that occupy the life created for them. Life is a strange mystery from this point of view here and now but has a completely different spiritual value to God. If we did not die then we could dig in our heels and build up stockpiles of gold and silver but we do die and we do move on. What will that person that dies physically do then? What value does this life have to the one that created it for us? This place is a spiritual proving ground for love. This life is a battlefield of love and hate. Which one will get the better of you? This place is a place for imperfect beings such as all of mankind to try and give and receive love in all its forms and situations. We are here to express love and give value to our spiritual selves in the after life. This world is this and much more. What is this world to you? Are you spirit first or flesh first? Is your love unconditional or are you filled with judgment and hatred for all others? It is not just important that you know the spiritual identity of Jesus; "Who do you say that you are?", is just as important a statement to make.

So let me ask you the hard questions

Do you value love or money, Hatred or love, good or evil?

Now let me ask you the real hard questions that will determine your destiny? Do you value giving a perfect love to others without any type of reward or do you simply love to be around people that love you that you love? Do you love those that love you? Do you love those that hate you? Are you interested more in what you give with no thought of reward or are you interested in what you get from others. These questions determine whom you walk with in the spiritual world while your physical body is alive in this world. God values the fact that God gives love with no expectation of someone returning love to God. When we return love to God that God gives us then the true miracles are created. It is no miracle that God can speak to any man, the miracle occurs when the man being spoken to obeys what is asked of him. The pathway to God starts with repentance. This concept started with John the Baptist and was fully fulfilled in the life and death and resurrection of Jesus. It is no miracle that God asks us to repent. The miracle is created when the man called to repentance turns his heart to repentance. Angels in heaven sing praises to God when a man repents, not before when God asks a man to repent. Our view of miracles is clouded. A true miracle of Jesus that goes over looked is that Jesus never once disobeyed the Father. Walking on water is a triviality compared to the fact that Jesus never once disobeyed the Father within the entire existence of Jesus.

I understand something about God now being back on earth . . .

THERE WILL ALWAYS BE A CONFLICT WITH THOSE THAT I SEEK TO HELP OR SHARE OR EVEN INTERACT WITH. PEOPLE ARE SELF-SERVING AND INDULGENT AND GOD GETS CAST OUT AT THE EARLIEST CONVENIENCE. MY LIFE IS DIFFERENT. I SERVE GOD FIRST AND SEEK NOT TO CAST GOD OUT OF SITUATIONS BUT HAVE GOD LEAD AND INSTRUCT THROUGH SITUATIONS IN LIFE. THIS SEEMS TO BE CAUSING CONFLICT WITH OTHERS. I SEEK TO DO THINGS FOR GOD AND THAT IS OK WHEN IT SERVES THOSE AROUND ME BUT WHEN IT DOES NOT SERVE THOSE AROUND ME AND ONLY SERVES GODS PURPOSE PEOPLE GET UPSET. MY ATTENTION IS DIVIDED BETWEEN GOD AND PEOPLE IN THE HERE AND NOW. HOW CAN ONE SPIRIT SERVE BOTH GOD AND PEOPLE WHEN PEOPLE SO WHOLE HEARTEDLY REFUSE GOD ON A DAY-BY-DAY SITUATIONAL CIRCUMSTANCE?

THIS IS THE DIVINE SERVICE TO GOD AND OTHERS CREATED BY GOD.

Having Faith vs. Being Faithful

What does this mean? Having faith means that you believe that Jesus can walk on water. Being faithful means that you love Jesus enough to not lie or cheat or steal or break the commandments. Being faithful means taking action and having the will and the courage to act on your own person faith. I hope and pray that we all may one day have both types of faith in our hearts. When we do, we will be closer to being complete for God.

5/14/2006

For some reason I have decided to start dating the entries that I make in this book since it has taken me several months to write and has taken me my entire life to live out. Some new things have come to mind and I thought that I might write down the new struggles that present themselves to me. This is what I go through and I suspect that others that have died and come back also go through this.

I want to do it again. Once was not enough. The more I learn about scripture and the more I read from the bible and all the other ancient texts I want to return to see what will be taught to me next. The more you learn the more you want to learn. The more you know about yourself the more you realize how empty you are and the more you want the emptiness within yourself to be filled. When you realize what you are lacking in your spirit you want to go in search of that which will fill the spirit.

This is the world of man, the physical man removed from God. This is the real of the Devil. There is nothing here in the world of man for me that is of God if I search for God and the true living being that is God and Son and Holy Spirit. I find areas of deficiency on me and areas of lacking and these are in the form of millions of unanswered questions. There are more questions than answers. So what does one do in this situation? Should I run off and try to die again? I have no idea. God does thing to me and with me but does not presume or even begin to hint of the possibility of making a choice for me. This is extremely frustrating at times. Sometimes, many times most of the time I need guidance and lots of it. I have come to the conclusion that I must be the dumbest most retarded child of God since I have seen so much and done so much and caused so much to happen and I still do not have the slightest clue as to what to do in many situations.

I struggle with the idea of throwing evil off the earth and throwing the devil out of heaven. I have found in many scriptures that the devil resides in heaven and stays there as the accuser of the brethren in Gods sight. Each man is given a measure of faith. The though of doing something significant like throwing the devil out of heaven excites me. I don't want to reside in the world as it is and simply wander through the rest of my days being resurrected accepting the injured and ill as they are. Children of God leave a wake of destruction to evil with every step that they take in their walk. Every day Jesus went out and destroyed evil. Jesus went out and restructured this world of man into the image of heaven and God. The greatest way to destroy evil is to change it. Giving sight to the blind was a way to destroy evil and the devils work. Allowing the lame to walk and the deaf to hear was not only a way of healing those that needed it but it has an underlying statement of taking this world and reshaping it to Gods will, not simply to allow this world to exist and do nothing about it.

Jesus tore down the devils handiwork in so many ways that go unnoticed. There are so many things that Jesus says with each step and action that he took and did that is so beautiful and so unnoticed by the average person. People simply do not take the time to look and listen to what is being said to them through action without words.

The question still remains will I do it again? I do not know yet. I am in Gods hands. If I do this again and get up and walk then I will complete this book and tell all within these pages. If I do it again and do not get up and walk then this will just become another lost mystery that will never be found or understood.

So let me tell you exactly what I have discovered in my readings of the bible. I have been studying the bible as it is and can be bought in the store and also other ancient texts such as the nag hammadi library of scriptures and other things such as all the early Christian writings on the internet and things like the gospel of peter and Thomas and Phillip. These writings make sense to me. These writings sound to me as if they were written by people that have died and been sent back. As I search through the Bible. I find texts within the book of revelations that the Spirit is bringing to my attention.

The passage that is being presented to me is this: Revelations 12:7-12:13

As I highlight this passage I don't want to rewrite it so take the time to look it up and I will explain what is being presented to me. I might speak in layman's terms so I could sound a little coarse.

Let me start at the beginning:

> God has crucified me.
> God has led me to my death during which God anointed me and called
>   me Son and Christ.
> God met with me in the after life out of this body.
> God resurrected me and could have placed me anywhere but chose to
>   put me back on earth.
> Now I am here faced with the dilemma of taking action. I see things
>   about earth that I do not like and see things in heaven that I do
>   not like and see things in hell that I do not like and it is a struggle
>   for me to decide how to act.

Should I die again and sacrifice myself to set foot into heaven and see the devil thrown down to earth? Should I die again and take a chance on going against Gods will for me? I have no desire to set my will against the will of God. Am I the One that has been chosen to do these things or am I chosen to simply know about these things. God did not anoint me with the hope that I would do nothing. God is a God of action. It infuriates me that the Devil may be in heaven with God arguing for this earth to continue the way it is while I must stay here and endure this agony along with countless others. Jesus succeeded. The lamb of God and his sacrifice was pure and occurred, things can change if only someone will come that will wield the weapon created by God for the purpose of destroying evil and the devil on earth. Is this me? Has God awoken me for this purpose along wih many other reasons? Is this my task at hand? Curiosity among other things is killing me to know but it is not the kind of question that can be answered through words, I need to die to find out. Death does not scare me, I know who created it. Not being able or willing to do Gods will is what scares me to no end. I have disappointed God for too long and it is my desire to no longer disappoint the Most High Living God.

Where am I now? My poison is ready. This time I will go for the whole pound of poison and not stop at 12 ounces. This time I have taken a blender and liquefied the entire solution and taken hard poison and put it in a blender and liquefied it into an elixir. The scent and taste of it is familiar to me. The question is this, is God with me and is God coaxing me? I spend much of my time praying about this and I receive the same invitation. COME AND SEE. I see them in heaven inviting me to act and to do. It is my life in spite of all the opinions of those that watch. It is my life and no one else's. I lay it down for whomever I choose. Agree or disagree with me, it is still my life and my choice. If I choose to lay it down for the almighty God that is everlasting and is unbegotten then so be it.

Whatever happens, if I choose to do this and come back I will write about it and will also bring witnesses this time to see me get up again if it is Gods will that I return to earth. I have found a friend that has courage enough to allow me to act on my faith and this person will be with me and watch what happens to me. This person will watch me die and watch me sacrifice myself for the living God that is above All. If I die again, and never return, then that person is instructed by me specifically to act as if they never new me. If I return then they will tell what they have seen to others. If I return then I will have something new to write about and the world is about to take a drastic turn for the worse.

I have burning questions about myself that I must know and only the living God and the one that has set me here can answer me in these matters. This is about me and my Father in Heaven and our relationship and this is about my following the path of the Christ that has walked the earth before my time. I follow Jesus searching for the Father and the Will of God for me. What will I find? Will I find myself lacking the courage to do this again? Will I be kept from returning and sharing the secrets that I discover? Will I not do this at all and choose a human life and remain earth bound and trapped with the boundaries this earth, which is leaning toward hell? I will see what I am. God will deal with me sooner or later. I hope to have the courage to do what God needs me to do and I hope to have the courage to see and to act upon what I see. I hope to see you soon God and I hope to see the Devil thrown from Your Heaven and I hope to return to tell the tale. I go to my death armed only with what is inside me and in my heart of hearts. You have said to me Come and See, perhaps I will. For this moment I will pray for the courage and the strength to see and to act upon what I see.

5/15/2006

I have been hard at prayer for almost and entire day now trying to find a sign within myself about what to do. Before I start to tell about what I did and found out I first want to state a few contradictions in my heart and these things are very difficult to overcome.

First and foremost I want to see Gods will done. I want to see Gods wishes granted. I want to see Gods desires filled.

I do not want to go against God and Savior any more in my life either through deliberate action or in-deliberate ignorance of Gods desires for me.

So here are the contradictions, I promised God I would not play with life and death anymore. I also promised God that my life is Gods to take if it is every needed.

Then I find a passage about Gods anointed and something that we are supposed to fulfill, which hints or includes dying deliberately for Gods purposes.

Recently I have been praying and something happened. God allowed me to see into heaven. I saw God and felt God inviting me to fulfill this scripture and to pray on this and help this scripture come to pass. Lets say that I felt a very, very strong invitation to come and see. So what do I do? All I have as a guide is the previous actions of God in my life to help. What I have been searching for is **a defining moment** in life that gives true concrete meaning to take action.

As I look back I still remember the taste and smell of the poison that I ate and several things occurred to me. I took the poison. I was not the one that healed me and I was not the one that made me immune to the poison. To put the whole occurrence in one sentence, God led me to take the poison so that I could see myself and see God. God led me to take it, then God watched me take it and them God healed me from taking it. That in essence is THE ALL. God is all-powerful over life and death and can lead you into it and out of it again without a scratch.

So I have come to the conclusion that if I were to take another pound of poison that it would be irrelevant. It would be and inert action. It would cause neither movement forward or backward in spirit.

So what did I do today while praying? I said many things and learned many things and saw many things and resurrection life has taken on a new dynamic or parameter or quest or search.

I offered God my life today once more. I took the liquefied poison and touched it to my tongue and said to God that if my life is required for the fulfillment of this prayer then so be it, these days of my life are the ones you have granted me anyway so they belong to you. I touched several drops of poison to my tongue and said I am not the one that is stopping this poison from doing its job, you are so once again here is my life. If you allow me to die then that is up to you but I will stand and say what I have to say about this passage that has come to mind. The truth is I hate this world the way it is and hate my life as it is without you so I will say what I have to say in regards to this passage in revelations.

God,

Jesus succeeded. The sacrifice of the Blood of the Lamb was pure and was true. The sacrifice that Jesus made for us is real. The Blood of the Lamb is Your weapon that You created for You to use against the Devil. If the Devil stands before you accusing the people of earth night and day as scripture says then I ask that the Blood of the Lamb and the Blood of Pure Innocence be put on the Devil. The Devil has created hell but has never stepped foot in it. The Devil creates chaos on earth but has never tasted that which the Devil has created. Let the Devil taste that which he has created. Let the Devil be thrown down to earth as scripture says. I offer You God, the Blood of our Savior as a weapon to use. I raise my hand to this God, as Moses raised his hand to part the sea and as Jesus raised his hand to call men back from the dead, I raise my hand to heaven and ask that the Devil be soaked in this Blood of Pure Innocence that was sacrificed for Us, your children. We have been made whole and pure in this Blood. What shall this Blood do to those that caused the need for this sacrifice to take place? What will this Blood do if it is thrown onto the Devil?

It is written that we, meaning mankind, were created to be above the angels and to have authority over the angels and as I stand in this Blood of Jesus I have faith that I am restored to what you God intended me to be. By this authority, this original intent of yours for Adam and authority over angels I ask that the Devil be thrown from heaven and cast down. I accept the Blood of Jesus for me and its healing power and all that it is, known and unknown. Can the Devil say the same thing? Cast this Demon that accuses mankind night and day down. Throw him down and have peace in Heaven and rejoice as it is written.

Throw this evil out of me as well. Drown me in the Blood of Jesus until the Devil in me is no more.

I prayed this prayer all day as the drops of poison took effect. Things that are not lethal have effect on me. These drops of poison are deadly I assure you and I do not recommend even touching the poison that I play with. Liquefying it and putting it on your skin allows your body to absorb it. I prayed this prayer all day today as I lay there severely tranquilized. I never fell asleep but did see two very strange things. I will try to describe the event as they happen so here is how it happens then here is what I saw. First imagine that you are lying there with your eyes closed and all you see is blackness, no images or shapes. You are awake and conscious. Your thoughts are your own and you are simply praying and opening your heart. Then all of a sudden the blackness drops away as if a curtain was being taken down and there was a view on the other side of the blackness. Now what you see is different every time but this is how it happens sometimes. I was lying there, awake my eyes were shut with a towel over my head to help keep out the daylight or room light and get complete blackness. Then it happened and I was allowed to see something. I saw a very large very powerful bolt of lightning hit the ground. It was a sustained bolt of lightning, meaning it did not hit and disappear. This bolt of lightning hit the ground and remained also connected to the sky and made a very loud noise. It was thicker than an average bolt of lightning and it also stayed longer than an average bolt of lightning and I also saw something else strange. A pulse of energy was traveling back up the bolt of lightning as if it were going up while the lightning was hitting the ground. This is the best that I can describe what I saw without making a computer-generated image and CGI cartoon about it. In short, as I prayed I saw a huge bolt of lightning strike the ground in a vision.

I also learned several other things about myself today that have nothing to do with battling the devil. I learned how ignorant I am of what God really want me to be and what God really wants me to do. I only saw God; I was not given infinite knowledge. Seeing what I saw strengthened my faith tremendously but I was not given any real advantage over this world yet.

A New Quest for Self Knowledge . . .

So now my quest has changed. I need to learn as much as I can about me and seek power over myself, not the world. I need to find the empty spaces of knowledge inside me and fill them as best I can through prayer and searching through scripture and going through experiences in the world with God in mind.

CHAPTER 7

REAL WORLD EVENTS, TEACHINGS AND PRACTICE AND PRINCIPLES . . .

Principles

Basic Spiritual Principles: I do not wish to attempt to rewrite the bible. I simply try and add a few other thoughts about things that I have learned in an attempt to confirm the bible and its teachings. Everything the bible has taught me has always worked to my spiritual advantage over evil itself, not over others.

Judge not or you will be judged

When we judge others we condemn ourselves to become that which we judge others to be. If you take a good look at people that surround you will notice that they have characteristics of what they condemn in others. If they do not have the characteristics of that which they condemn in others, they soon will.

Gods plan is for us to forgive. When God places us in a situation that forces us to become that which we condemn in others then we learn the need for forgiveness.

What I will describe to you is a real life situation that some or perhaps all of us are guilty of doing or committing: This is a non-gender problem both genders are guilty.

A man or woman can end up thinking of him or herself, as perfect and can do no wrong. A spouse marries a spouse and blames the other spouse for everything and admits nothing that was done wrong in the relationship. The one spouse accuses the other spouse and condemns the other spouse and still admits he or she can do no wrong and believes that he or she did nothing wrong. The problems of the marriage were the other entire spouses fault and the accusing spouse blames the other spouse for everything then subsequently leaves that marriage in ruins and everything collapses. This person; being man or women, never once thought of their own actions as doing anything bad. While in the marriage all that person did was hurt and break the heart of the spouse on a daily basis and never realized their own actions, all the one spouse did was accuse others for their problems and internal pain.

Now lets compare this self-proclaiming perfect man to the real perfect man known as Jesus. Jesus never once condemned anyone and he was perfect. Jesus, if Jesus ever did anything that needed an apology would have been honest enough to admit it and apologize although Jesus never had to walk that path. Self-proclaiming self-made perfect people always tend to condemn others and never themselves. Jesus could see all our sins from beginning to end and never once condemned anyone, in fact, Jesus died so we could live. Jesus died so the self-righteous could be made righteous. So think of this when people accuse you of things. Jesus never condemned us; he was the only man without sin against God. We do not have the right and are not right if we condemn others. We can only be responsible for our own actions.

FEAR

Yeah though I walk through the valley of the shadow of death **I will fear no evil** for thou art with me . . . .

Distinct characteristics of God and things from God and the devil . . .

What does fear itself do to you? How is trust involved?

Demons try to invoke fear in others and God asks for trust in God when fearful things or situations arrive.

Evil uses negative emotions such as fear, doubt and many other things to keep you from showing, releasing or acting upon your faith or accepting the will of God and Gods gifts for you.

SEX VERSUS WAITING
THIS IS HARD FOR EVERYONE
CLOTHES ON AGAINST CLOTHES OFF

It's even harder for someone to stop this once they have practiced it for years and years. Lets state a few facts: Our society is disposable. If you aren't satisfied and there is no instant gratification then get rid of it.

What does our society teach as opposed by bible teachings?

We all know what the bible teaches and we immediately and instinctively reject it without even thinking that it might be the exact way to go. Rejection of principles is a common downfall for most.

What are the benefits of simply taking the time to get to know someone before jumping in the sack with someone? If you have been living the lifestyle of hitting the hay before you look to the good book then you may have already answered your question and don't know it. Sex is not love. Sex is not relationship. You can physically have sex with anyone but you can't get along with everyone. We are all not compatible or interchangeable. If we were universally compatible and universally interchangeable then more people would stay together. People have sex first then find out later, I just really don't like this person or the fun has worn off or whatever. What an unstable love we have without Gods help to stabilize our hearts and minds within him.

It is no coincidence that so many marriages are ending up in divorce because of this simple thing, sex before marriage, we are taught that everything is disposable and if we encounter the slightest problem that really involves effort or forgiveness then just throw it away and start over. People want it all but don't give their all, they give nothing but want everything. Then when the hearts start breaking people start calling on God. If God would have been consulted and obeyed from the beginning then things might have worked out.

Let me say this in another way it is no coincidence that when people do the exact opposite of the bible they fail miserably and end up broken. Marriage takes two people following the same book following the same God doing what the instructions say. Do things your own way and see what happens.

Common denominators of relationships falling apart, Things that I have noticed:

Relationships do not fall apart due to situations in the world or exterior forces. Relationships fall apart due to the heart and keeping promises and internal problems. Let your yes mean yes and no mean no.

The Downfall of Relationships

I have noticed that people say this at some point and then sooner or later their relationship falls apart. It starts like this . . . "I don't think this is going to work out . . ." at some point there is one spouse that says this to the other spouse.

What kind of person says lets get married then some time later they say to their spouse I don't think this is going to work? This is not yes meaning yes and no meaning no. This person is not self aware enough to understand the problem that was just invoked into their lives. What kind of person gets people to do something with them and then decides that after they get what they want such as marriage that they decide its not going to work out. Who has the right to play with other people in this manner?

There are 2 kinds of relationships with other people, a relationship that includes Jesus as the center of that person's life and a relationship with a person that does not have Jesus as the center of their life. I can tell you that I have been both types of these people and I wish that I could go back and make Jesus the center of my life then go and meet all the people that I met in the course of my life.

Jesus is Salvation. What does Jesus save us from? Jesus saves us from ourselves among many other things. I have been a person selfish without God as the center of my life. It is no fun to be that way and no fun to be associated with that type of person. If you decide to love someone that is Godless in his or her life then this is a testament to your open heart and your love, this is not a testament to the quality of the person that you love. God loves us before salvation just as much as when we are saved.

Anyway there is a whole other book about God, it's called the Bible perhaps you might consider reading it, going to church once in awhile instead of saying how you can't go because of all the backsliding Christians there and go and see God for yourself and let God into your life. Relationship principles are completely detailed in the bible and I'm not going to try and re-list them here. The bible says things completely and perfectly if you take the time, meaning your lifetime to understand them.

Here are just some other thoughts of things that can destroy a relationship that are seldom considered to be dangerous.

Contempt and familiarity, after you commit to someone you start to feel comfortable and relax into a possible false sense of security.

Forgetting the little things, thank you for being here, let me get the door, say I love you before you go to bed, thank you for trying so hard to provide even if failure occurs.

When you stop growing and learning new things that keep two hearts close and together.

Appreciate what you have and do not beat up each other over what you do not have.

Your fortune is found in the heart of those that truly love you,
not in your wallet. How can you tell those that truly love you; the one that
truly loves you will never condemn you in any state of being that you are in
while in this life, when you are the worst person that you can be,
they will still be brave enough and dare to say

I STILL LOVE YOU.

About Marriage . . . .

Everything that is wonderful about marriage is done while the clothes are still on your body. It is a joy to come home to someone after a hard, long days work and find them there, waiting with a kiss and a warm smile and love in their heart.

Sex is just sex and will become more empty with each passing day and the pleasure of it will be gone when a spirit decides to shift inside itself and start to thirst and hunger for true love of the heart. Then all the sex in the world will not satisfy you and you will become numb.

It is a wonderful feeling to know that you are working to provide for those that you love in your heart and this working for those that you love gives meaning and purpose to your life and the work that you do. Providing for those that you love gives a wonderful sense of purpose to those that provide.

Working for nothing is more tiring than the actual work that is done! Working for nothing will be a weight upon the spirit and make each step while working seem like impossible movements. To work in vain and for nothing is worse than the hardest labor you can find.

It is a wonderful thing to sit and wash the dishes and clothes and sweep the floor and fix the house because all these things are there to be used to provide for the ones that you love.

When the house becomes more important than the ones that dwell within it then all is lost. You will know how wonderful it is to wash dishes when you have no dish to wash or place to wash it in. When the size, square footage and the financial value of the home becomes more important than the quality of the relationship that occur within the structure then the marriage is lost.

It is a pure joy to have the woman or man that you love, come home to a dinner prepared for him or her by the husband or wife. It is a joy to watch the other person be satisfied and eat. They are not eating food; they are eating and feasting on the love in the heart of the person that has provided for them.

When you come home to a house where no one waits for you it is like coming home to a desert place with loneliness for friends and empty chairs with no one to sit in them. There are no flowers that bloom in the human heart that can survive in a desert waist land of loneliness.

There are really only a few things to do in marriage, eat, sleep, work, clean, organize and remain in control of finances, repair the house, repair the vehicles and all the daily chores that are needed. There are other things to do as well; these things are things of the spirit such as sharing in each other's hearts and love and simply appreciating the fact that the other person is there. Growing together, growing pure love in ones heart and keeping close through any circumstance and situation, these are the things that make a marriage wonderful.

Get married and become strangers. Make sure that you separate yourself from your spouse as often as you can. Say I love you but make sure that you lie when you say it. Leave the other person alone and defenseless when there is a problem. Become selfish and cheat the other person out of their happiness. Do all these things then justify your actions and tell the world how you are always right. Get your divorce and enjoy it.

A true wife and a true husband can say, "I am wrong ", before they find fault with the other person. I am sorry, I love you and I was wrong are the things that should be said.

If you spend your time telling the other person their faults and problems and never admit your own then the relationship is lost. If you cannot say you are sorry or I love you or I am wrong then you will have the privilege of watching your heart and the heart of the one that you love turn to stone if it was not that way in the beginning.

It gives life to a relationship to know that you are appreciated for all your toil and labor and rest and it gives life to appreciate a person for all that they do even if they do not succeed in anything that they venture after to acquire. It gives life to be able to give and receive appreciation. If you agree and this is true then the opposite must take life away.

Do not appreciate a person and show no appreciation for anything and each day becomes a brick in a wall that is built and one day you will never be able to touch that person's heart even when you can hold their hand. Watch how that person slowly dies in front of you.

Knowing that you have tomorrow is one of the greatest gifts that a husband and a wife can give to each other. Do you know how to give the gift of tomorrow? When you decide to get married that is what you give to each other, the gift of always having tomorrow, no matter what today may bring, you always have tomorrow. Tomorrow will have many gifts inside if it when it is properly unwrapped. Apologies, solutions to problems and making amends for hurtful things said and done come wrapped inside tomorrow. If tomorrow never comes then these things may be lost.

An expectation of perfection is one of the deadliest things that a person can have in their heart for another person. Expect a person to be perfect and expect disappointment. Expect a person to be perfect and watch how YOU become more imperfect and less forgiving to everyone. We must learn to accept people where they are in their growth in life, especially the ones that we commit a relationship of marriage together.

YOUR TREASURE CAN BE FOUND IN THE HEART OF ONE THAT LOVES YOU NOT IN YOUR WALLET OR BANK. IT IS KNOWN THAT RICH PEOPLE DIVORCE AND RICH

PEOPLE COMMIT SUICIDE AND THEIR MONEY NEVER KEPT THEM SAFE FROM THESE THINGS.

SHARED EXPERIENCES ARE A FORTUNE ALL THEIR OWN AND SHARED MEMORIES WITH THOSE THAT ARE TRULY LOVED CANNOT BE BOUGHT.

WHO DECIDES IF THESE THINGS ARE GOING ON IN YOUR RELATIONSHIP, YOU DO . . . .

Selfless Behavior versus Selfish Behavior

Both types of behavior cause others to be led into judgment of others.

Selfless behavior: I notice this in others after practicing selfless behavior, people watch in amazement at a person that gives to others with no thought to ones self. This causes others to step out in their actions and begin to take care of the person with the selfless behavior. Someone selfless causes and leads others into taking care of the one that is selfless. This behavior is a mystery to those that are preoccupied with selfishness. The selfish person is quick to condemn a selfless person. A caring person whom is being taken care of by the selfless person is quick to come forward and return kindness for kindness and become selfless. This creates a balance of need beings satisfied on the spiritual level and also creates a place in their hearts where trust and love can grow. This also creates a symbiotic relationship of mutual dependence. This is the manner in which God wants us dependent on each other and also completely dependent on God and Gods wisdom and love. Selfless behavior causes barriers to be broken and brought down, communication to grow and open up and all manner of life to flow between two people.

Selfish behavior causes others to be judgmental and condemning to that person. The selfish person thinks only of them self and others around them are conditioned to expect this action. Selfish people consider their own interests before others and consider their own interests above the value of property of others. Thus life and all things are devalued and selfishness rises to the surface. Selfish behavior causes conflict because the needs of others in a family type arena are not being met. Selfishness causes conflict on all levels because the selfish people can seldom see past themselves to see or meet the need of those around them. This can occur in a mild or extreme extent depending on how far the selfish person is willing to go with their personal appetite for selfishness. Selfishness causes ones focus to become on their internal self thus creating their own form of idol worship and this results in losing sight of God. This type of behavior is spoken against in all its forms throughout the bible.

Free will versus Gods will

God's will brings miracles.
God's will brings salvation.
God's will brings all things of God into our hearts.

Free will . . .

Free will brings nothing but lack of all these things listed above. Why is free will considered to be a gift instead of a curse? There is only one thing to do with free will and freely and willingly give it back to God and say that you don't want it. What man among us can create a miracle from their free will without God? What man can save himself from damnation without God? What man has the power to bring to himself and into himself all things of God without God?

Free will is an illusion created by the lie of disobedience created in the Garden. Free will is an illusion created when one loses sight of God and others. Obedience to God creates life and love and the lack of lies and deceit and darkness why would one seek to fight against this and not give up all to have this? Obedience to Gods will does not make a person less it makes a person more. God has free will and is the only one responsible enough to have this ability and not bring himself to ruination with free will. Free will has always brought destruction to anyone that seeks to use or impose his or her free will upon others. Think of your own life, when has free will ever served you correctly or when has it brought about destruction. Some choices that are bad cant be seen for many years until it is too late. Free will creates the illusion of self thus creating idol worship and all other types of sin against God. In heaven there is no such thing as free will. They all do Gods will in heaven. No one in heaven wants free will, why do we fight for it so vigorously here. The earth is below heaven according to scripture.

There is only one truth. There is no variation of this one truth. The one true truth is a living breathing being that has a will. When a person learns of this one true truth that is alive they must obey that truth thus giving up free will.

IF FREE WILL IS SUCH A GIFT AND BLESSING THEN WHY DOES GOD ALWAYS AND CONSISTENTLY ASK US TO DENY OUR

OWN FREE WILL TO SERVE GOD AND OTHERS? JESUS DENIED
HIMSELF AND HIS OWN BEST INTEREST TO THE GREATER
GOOD FOR OTHERS AND TO BE OBEDIENT TO GODS WILL.
WHAT IS BEING SAID TO YOU IN THEIR ACTIONS? CONSISTENTLY
THROUGHOUT THE HISTORY OF THE BIBLE WHEN PEOPLE
DISOBEYED GOD THEY FEEL FROM GODS SERVICE, FAVOR,
MIRACLES AND BLESSINGS. FREE WILL IS NOT A GIFT IT IS A
WEAPON THAT WE CANNOT WIELD. IF ONE CAN'T IMAGINE
LIFE WITHOUT IT, THEN THIS PERSON CANNOT IMAGINE A
TRUE LIFE WITH GOD.

**Other thoughts about free will, here is something that
I have noticed in behavior of people in their spirituality.**

If you walk up to someone and tell them to stop doing something that is self
destructive such as drinking and smoking cigarettes the first thing that comes out
of their mouth is a confession about their free will and they have a RIGHT to
smoke and drink and do whatever and they argue for the right to do things that
are damaging. Now here is the interesting thing and the counter point.

Whenever a person has a real problem that they are facing and they feel like they
want to run away and they can't handle the situation they start praying to God
and the exercising of the free will over the situation is abandoned. People fight to
do things self destructive with their free will but when it comes time to exercise
the free will in their life to control a circumstance or situation in life they turn
tail and run. Think about your life and see if you have ever done this.

So here is the question that you should be asking, do you control the circumstances
or do the circumstances control you? Do you control your feelings or do your
feelings control you? Do you control the problem and handle the problem or
does the problem control you?

Now if you are saying things to yourself like, I need to leave this area, I want
to go back home, I'm not happy, I hate this place meaning the location of my
life . . . etc . . . it means that you are not doing what you need to do and you are
not exercising your free will in the manner in which it is meant to be used. Free
will is not an excuse to go out and defile your body, it is a tool that can be used
to control you life situations and keep destruction to a minimum or non-existent
in your life. Learn to make good choices that keep destruction to a minimum or
non-existent in your life.

People fight for their free will when it gives them a chance to self-destruct but when it comes to making a free will choice that is constructive then life becomes and impossibility and people do not know how to use their free will.

Of their own free will women put babies in dumpsters. Of their own free will people allow their emotions to lead them to murder. Of their own free will people lie and cheat and steal. Of their own free will women sell their bodies and sex for money and drugs. Of their own free will people abuse and neglect the ones the profess to love and care for.

Exercising your free will to stop doing self-destructive things is rare. People seldom stop to give the man on the corner a sandwich or pick him up and take him into their home. As a society we are content to let other sleep in the street and starve. We tell ourselves lies that make us feel better about choices that we know to be wrong. We make a choice to leave the man outside on the street and starve after that follows excuses as to why it is ok to do this so we tell ourselves reassurances that are lies, if you were out there, you would want someone to help and rescue you.

A hint about God and the Devil

If a voice tells you "Don't do that" please don't do it. Chances are that it is God trying to stop you from doing something harmful to yourself or others. If God takes the time to tell you not to do something for your own good then please listen. If you do then you will in fact be more faithful to God than I have ever been.

Most of the time the Devil leads you to do things and says go ahead and do it. If it feels good do it. Think about it and you may see in your life how many times the devil and God have spoken to you.

Strange events and a pattern of characteristics emerge . . . .

In the past few months while writing this book I have been studying the bible, philosophy, lost scriptures, videos of other resurrections and real world events concerning Angels. I have noticed that a pattern is presenting itself to me and it is very apparent throughout scripture. I have noticed a pattern in behavior in God that is very interesting and very difficult to put into words. I will start by making a statement and this statement is true for my life as well as true about the pattern of events that I have noticed. Here it is.

GOD NEVER TELLS ME WHAT TO DO . . .

Now why do I make this statement and where am I getting my reasoning? I pray, you pray we all pray from time to time and there is always a burning question that we all ask and say to God from time to time, Just go ahead and tell me what I am supposed to do God. Tell me what to do God because I can't figure it out for myself. However for some reason God seldom if never actually tells us exactly what to do. As I look back at my life God has always shown me the outcome of events in my life through supernatural dreams. I have always seen the future events that surround choices **that I have made**. God never would tell me what to do; God would simply show me the outcome of events that were caused by the choices that I have made or will make if you believe that God has the power to show you the future. God has shown me my own personal future many times and now after seeing this, questions come to mind, profound questions that cannot be answered by anyone other than God. God showed me my future and the events that would transpire, now did God show me what God wanted me to do or did God show me what would happen due to the choices that I made or will make.

GOD DOES THINGS BUT NEVER
GIVES INFORMATION . . .

There was a man other than myself that died and was given a tour of heaven and hell. He was sent back to earth and felt that it was needed to tell everyone that he met about what he saw and what happened to him. This man had an Angel for a guide and the Angel took him on a tour and showed him things but never gave any information about what the man was viewing. The Angel took the man to heaven and to the house that Jesus is building, if you know your bible then you know about what I'm talking about, the Angel took the man to Hell and allowed him to stand there and simply get a good view.

Now, lets take a reverse look at what happened. The Angel took the man places but never offered any definition about what was being shown. For example imagine that I take you to the beach and then to a river and then to a desert and then took you on a boat to the middle of the ocean and imagine also that I would never say a word to you. So I take you places and show you things but real information about what is being viewed is not given. It is as if we are allowed or are being shown things and then are expected to extrapolate our own ideas and make up our own mind with no outside influence. God does things to me like heals me and loves me and often speaks to me about other people so that I may give them a helping hand but God never tells me exactly what to do in any given specific information. This is a great gap in our relationship. We have an internal desire to know the mind of God. We have this, it is built into us, even though we may or may not be conscious of it. The Ten Commandments are also like this. The commandments are directives of what not to do, not what we should do.

The Angels of Mons . . .

During World War One there was an event that made national news. It was called the battle of Mons and real life Angels intervened and stopped the fighting of this battle. Many soldiers were rescued and saved from dying. This event can be researched on the internet for the full story. Basically there was a battle during WW1 and several Angels of God stepped in and literally stopped the shelling and bombing and rifles and allowed the soldiers to walk back to the rear lines and be saved.

Now what am I trying to point out. Action was taken but explanation was not given. The Angels never told the people that they saved why they were saved but the angels did allow those particular soldiers to see them with their physical eyes. The soldiers came back to the rear camp completely in awe of what they had seen.

What else am I trying to point out? The Angels could have done this any time they wanted to and stopped the war all together. They chose to stop that particular battle and that particular situation. They acted but gave no explanation. What was so important about those particular soldiers and not that other millions that died in war? This speaks to me of manipulation without explanation. It has gone on through out history. There are unseen forces that have been manipulating everything and have intervened from time to time and we are sometimes allowed to see this.

What am I trying to point out? God acts but seldom gives explanation or information. God prevented a friend of mine from falling to his death in a pile of debris of a building. I friend of mine was working 3 to 4 stories in the air and fell of the building into a pile of rubble and stood up without a scratch. Another friend of mine also fell off a building about 3 stories up and said that he landed directly on his feet and nothing happened to him. This happened in front of witnesses. He described this event to me as taking a ride with God that day.

God acted and God did something but God did not offer any direction or explanation as to why their life was spared at that moment and God also did not say what they were supposed to do with their life. So as the saying goes the mystery gets deeper. What does this knowledge say to you? What presents itself to you and what jumps out to you?

SIN, MY CURRENT DEFINITION ...

A friend of mine recently asked me to explain my definition of the word sin and what do I think that sin is. I found my answer to be interesting so I thought that I would put it down somewhere in these pages. I read the bible with a dictionary. Even the simplest of words can be misleading. I also have learned that we are ever changing and ever evolving in thought and internal knowledge so my deep, deep definition of sin today will be a shallow version tomorrow as I grow up and out. As we grow our personal definition of things change and become larger along with our intellect.

The word SIN means without. A sinner is not an action or a do or do not; it is a state of being just like happy or sad or joy. Sin means without, but without what? A sinner is without knowledge. A sinner is a person that is in a state of being without knowledge. Our state of being directs our actions. So a person without knowledge commits acts that are flawed and also does not know why they should stop doing what they are doing. A person that is without knowledge about lying will continually lie and does not know why they should stop lying, lack of knowledge leads to destruction, personal destruction. So the question is can you see where this is leading? A sin is not something that we do or do not do, a sinner is a state of being without knowledge as to why they should not lie or cheat or steal or kill. This state of being leads people to continue to do these things. A lack of knowledge as to why you should not lie or steal allows you to believe that it is ok to do these things and so people do them. People lie and cheat and steal and kill.

Sin or a sinner is a state of being and the act that a sinner commits or does is a byproduct or affirmation of that state of being or a fruit, a lie is a fruit of the labor of a being that is in a state of a lack of knowledge. To put things in reverse, someone that knows why they should not lie or cheat or steal or kill does not do these things and they also know WHY they should not do these things and also does not seek to put him or herself in this type of situation where the temptation to do these things will occur.

Do bad things happen to us randomly or do you invite disaster through choice?

Are there coincidences in life or is this world created?

Are you causing your own problems or using your free will to prevent problems in your life? We suffer through our choices.

View of the Bible while the book is closed lying on the table . . .

Before Dying, I viewed the bible in a very physical way. I viewed the bible from a view of the flesh. Each line that I read was interpreted for my spirit by the flesh. In my heart I understood the bible as the flesh understands it. This is a "lost soul" point of view and a "lost" definition of the Bible. The view of the flesh is a wrong view and wrong interpretation of the Bible. I once understood this book as it was defined for my by my physical senses and physical values or fleshly values, which I now understand to be wrong.

The Bible is a book about spirit. It is a book about Gods spirit and our spirit and reuniting all of our spirits with God. This reuniting can take place on earth or in heaven. The Bible is a book about Spirit not flesh. To interpret something that is from the spirit and about the needs of the spirit in a fleshly manner is a recipe for disaster. Spirit feeds Spirit. I see things through eyes of the spirit and try to look at things as if I were a spirit not from the point of view of this tiny little body that my spirit is residing within.

After Dying, I see things differently now. I think of myself as spirit first and flesh last and hope to see things as if the flesh does not exist and I do not reside within it. I look for the spiritual meaning that is found within each line of text that is written with the Bible and not the physicality of it. These two separate and distinct views will determine what you find within its pages before you even open the book. Are you flesh looking for fleshly values or are you spirit looking for spiritual values.

Bible plus dictionary equals success in understanding

One of the most powerful things that I have learned recently about the bible is that you should never read the bible without a dictionary. Recently I have been studying all texts and all different versions of the bible. We are being misled; we are misleading ourselves with shallow interpretations and shallow understandings of words.

I will give one example to try and show you what I am talking about here. I want you to think of your current definition of the word adultery. Keep in mind what you think that it means. Now let me write for you the true definition of the word adultery and adulterate.

Adulterate: To corrupt, debase or make impure of an admixture of a foreign substance . . . .

So how does this match up to your shallow meaning of the word adultery? This means that when you adulterate a relationship you are making your relationship impure by adding ingredients that corrupt its purity such as lying. A relationship is not sex. Sex is an action or something that is done. Applying the definition of Adultery that you find here to the commandment, thou shall not commit adultery; a completely new, broad-spectrum definition is discovered. There is also something else that people never take into consideration. We think that the commandments apply to how we treat each other but never take into consideration that they apply to how we treat and approach God and how we interact and relate with God. Thou shall not commit adultery against the lord thy God. Do not adulterate your relationship with God, as well as your relationship with other people.

God, accountability, sin and the Commandments

This touches base on a completely new concept that aligns other concepts of accountability. What if all the commandments are not directed to how we treat each other as we assume. What if the commandments are directed as to how we treat God, **first** and foremost in our lives **and then** they apply to how we treat each other.

> Thou shall not lie to the Lord thy God.
> Thou shall not steal from lord thy God.
> Thou shall not murder for the lord thy God.
> Thou shall not commit adultery toward the lord thy God.
> Thou shall not covet thy neighbor's wife and everything else thy
> neighbor owns in the sight of the lord thy God.
> Thou shall not bear false witness against thy neighbor in the presence
> of the lord thy God.

Now to get the entirety of each commandment you must look up Exodus and see the complete commandment as it is written and if you read it closely it is worded as to how you will treat God first, not how you treat other people as if God does not exist.

We always assume that the commandments are and were directed or are directives as to how we will treat each other. What happened to God? Did God just vanish suddenly? Did God cease to exist? It only makes sense that the commandments were designed to keep us close to God and keep us within the boundaries of our Father in Heaven by not doing these things to God. We always look at breaking a commandments as what we do to each other but what does it do to our relationship with God and what does it do to our accountability of our sins? We are not held accountable for the sins that are done to us. We are not responsible for pointing out other people's sins. We are held accountable for the sins that we commit. So what does this do to your knowledge? Does it add to or subtract from your previous thoughts about the commandments? Adding to your knowledge and broadening your spectrum of knowledge is always a sign that it is something from God. Now I need to Go pray that God give me the strength and ability and resolve to keep Gods commandments in regards to my relationship with God on a day-by-day, minute-by-minute outlook in my life.

SEVEN THINGS YOU NEED TO KNOW . . .

WHO, WHAT, WHERE, WHEN, WHY, HOW AND FAITH . . . .

There are two kinds of faith; the first is blind faith and blind trust. The type of faith that is blind in nature is also a faith that is without knowledge. This faith is simple, raw and pure. God always loves this type of faith. The second kind is of faith is an educated faith. This type of faith knows the seven things listed above, the who, the what, the where, the why, the when, the how and the faith or what you believe.

When you know all aspects of a situation you have an ability to act on your faith in an educated manner. If you do not know one of these 7 things then there is a blind spot in any given situation. Let me use the words of our Savior as an example. **Jesus said** that if a man have two coats let him give one away and if a man would steal your coat offer him your shirt as well.

These are some very radical statements to be making, especially when you know that the people that you talk to are selfish and self centered. Now if you do not know who or what or where or when or why or how Jesus is telling us to do these things then your faith will be blind and confused and you will not know what to do. This is an example as to why it is important to know all aspects of circumstance and situation and also the person that you are involved with.

After knowing all these things what happens is that a knowledge is formed inside you and you have a real ability to protect yourself from others and from situations that seem harmful.

The next plateau above the who, the what, the where, the when, the why and the how and the faith is the ability to make and effective concrete stable change. This is the ability to change ones self and ones environment for the better.

Lets put this into a humanistic or personal example. I will start with faith. I will use a drug addict as an example because the cause and effect are obvious. A drug addict acts on their faith. A drug addict believes that it is ok to do drugs and perpetuate their addiction. If a person believed that it was not ok to do this they simply do not do it and escape the addiction. Now lets expand this philosophy and you can actually put a blank where the word drug addict is and fill it in yourself with whatever problem that you are dealing with. A_____ acts on their faith. A _____ believes that it is ok to _____. This is how the word faith is a major part of the W.W.W.W.W.H and faith scenario. A drug addict does not know WHO they are hurting or WHY they should stop doing this. A drug addict does not know WHERE to begin if they wish to stop. A drug addict does not know HOW to stop. Now, when a drug addict sees something bad and an external catalyst occurs that makes them say that it is not OK for them to keep doing this then they start to believe that it might not be OK to do this and then the change occurs and the search for the W.W.W.W.W.H, and faith happens. So then something strange occurs, in their search for knowledge this person finds all these answers to questions then finds the ability to act and finds the strength (praying to God for it) to change their life and stop doing drugs. I have encountered many pastors and preachers that have been saved or delivered from drugs and I do not think that they realize that this is the path that they walked but I suspect that in looking back and reading what I write here they might agree with me that this is what happened to them. Now in reading my book, you might be on a search fro knowledge that might help empower you to conquer something. Look for the answers to these questions and you might find something that you need along the way and then have an ability to make effective change. Do not forget God. Ask and pray along the way. Do what you are told and listen when you ask. for answers. Sometimes find an answer requires paying attention to the situation not to the spoken word that you might hear.

Knowing these seven things will never hurt, it will only give you more insight and more information about any given situation and then your ability to see into that situation for a path might present itself. A major prayer and a major problem that we all have the believe and for those of us that choose to walk the path of God is, "What to do." We all constantly ask what should I do, what do you want me to do God what is a correct course of action to take here in this situation. This philosophy is a good beginning to apply to any situation. After you find the who and what and where and when and why and how your faith might just change and could have possibly gone through several changes. The question after this is will you have the courage to act on what you believe? I guess it is really up to you, if you are suffering by your own hands are you educated enough to be able to stop or do you simply wish to continue to suffer? Are you suffering and do not even know it?

THE PERFECT BEING OF GOD

We all know God to be a perfect being. I have recently learned that our human limited concept of perfection is not what the true perfection of God is in reality.

The best way that I can describe God's perfection is compare God to you. Look back at your life and imagine all the promises that you have made to other people and look at all the promises that you have never kept. Imagine if you had the ability to keep every single promise that you made and imagine that you had the discipline to make promises and keep them. Imagine that you had the ability to see promises that you could not keep so you simply would not make promises that you would not keep.

Now try to imagine God. God has kept every single promise that God has every made to every single spirit that God has promised anything. God is eternal and has no beginning or end. Imagine keeping promises for that time and never missing or failing to keep one promise. This is the true perfection of God, simple plain consistency with what is spoken to others. Now imagine a being also that has never told any type of lie. That is much harder to understand since we, caught in the human condition feel that it is necessary for the little white lie to exist.

SPIRITUAL VALUE ...

I have often wondered what exactly does God value? We all know we are not worthy and should go to hell. This gives me a burning question that I would really like to see the answer to sometime soon. What is it exactly, specifically; precisely that God loves about us? We can all look at each other and see that we are no good up to no good and we all tell each other to go to hell on a daily basis. So what is it that God sees in us that is so special that Jesus would die for us? I hope and suspect that one day we will all know the answer to this and I suspect that it is going to be found in the secret of our own personal salvation.

I still have the question and the quest that drives me to discover what it is that heaven values. I would like to share with you my most recent encounter with the Holy Spirit and the complete story is written about in chapter 10 of this book but I want to point out a few things that fall into line with the concept of spiritual value and what is valued by God and heaven and Jesus.

From the pages of Luke 21 and Mark 12:41
The widow and her 2coins . . .

There were people giving at the temple and a widow walked up and placed 2 coins in the container that carried the items and Jesus pointed out that what this woman was more valuable than what the other people gave because of the spirit in which she gave, not because of the monetary amount that she gave. The widow simply gave all the she had and left herself nothing even to live off of or get food for the day. This is a profound statement and goes over looked as to the true value of what we reap and sow in this world.

THIS WAS AN ACT OF TRUE SELFLESS LOVE THAT JESUS POINTED OUT AND IS WHAT IS TRULY VALUED IN HEAVEN

In Chapter 10 . . . Jeff and Lesley . . .

While I was watching Jeff and looking for what God was going to show me about Jeff it was shown to me that during Vietnam a man had died in Jeffs arms and that man spoke to me straight across the threshold or barrier that exists between Heaven and Earth and told me to specifically thank Jeff for the fact the Jeff was willing to sacrifice himself for that person that is in heaven right now.

Jeff ran into enemy gunfire to rescue a fellow soldier that moments later died in Jeff's arms.

So what was really said to me? In order to see this you must see the entire spectrum of possibilities of things that could have been said to me about Jeff and **were not** and then you must see the one thing that **was said to me** about Jeff and there in lies the secret to spiritual value.

Jeff's act of selfless behavior is what is valued in heaven. The fact that Jeff gave no thought or regard to himself was the one thing that was pointed out to me and not anything else.

Here is the spectrum, of Gods choices that God could have personally spoken to me. God could have told me to leave Jeff alone; there is no helping him. God could have pointed out all the horrific things that Jeff did during the war and had me convict him of many horrors that he did. God could have said nothing and not gotten involved. There are hundreds of choices that God could have taken and made in Gods personal involvement in that moment but this one act should stand out.

God chose to show me that Jeff is forgiven. That is why no single negative thing about Jeff's life on earth was pointed out to me. This man Jeff was a true hero in many ways and God also showed me this person that is in heaven right now and God told me to share with Jeff a personal thank you from that person in heaven to Jeff here on earth.

Thank you for trying to rescue me. Thank you for putting yourself in danger and the complete disregard that you had for yourself in those moments. Thank you for coming back for me. Thank you is being spoken in a way that words cannot even begin to articulate.

THIS WAS AN ACT OF TRUE SELFLESS LOVE THAT GOD POINTED OUT AND IS WHAT IS TRULY VALUED IN HEAVEN

From the pages of Matthew 9:37
The harvest is plentiful but the workers are few. Ask the Lord of the harvest to send workers out into the field.

This is a parable that I never rally understood and I believe that this is what is truly being said in the parable.

Who are the laborers? What is the Harvest? Why are the laborers few? What is the item of the Harvest being gathered?

The laborers are those people that love God and are willing to commit selfless acts of love in this world of selfishness. The Harvest is the selfless love that is created in that Act of selfless love. The Harvest is gathered in ones personal afterlife in the THANK YOU that is given back in heaven. The person that received that act of selflessness here on earth is the one giving back to the person doing that act of selfless behavior in heaven. WE do someone an act of selfless love here on earth and there is a very substantial reward that exists in Heaven and is waiting in Heaven. The harvest being gathered is living breathing love that is created within acts of selfless love and is what is harvested and valued in Heaven. The Acts of selfless love are taking place on earth with no seeming value or reward but when that soul reaches heaven there is a thing of living breathing love waiting there. The harvest (in Heaven) is a harvest of selfless giving love from a land (earth) that is barren of people that love in a selfless manner.

From the testimonies of the people that experienced an NDE . . .

A large majority of people that have had and NDE experience say that we are in this world to perfect our ability to love one another without hesitation or reservation and also without condition. We are to perfect our ability to give unrestrained unconditional love to each other without any thought of reward. This documented over and over in testimony after testimony of people that have died and been returned. I have heard this in many videos also.

THERE WERE ACTS OF TRUE SELFLESS LOVE THAT GOD POINTED OUT TO THE N.D.E. PERSON IN THEIR LIFE REVIEW AND THIS IS WHAT IS TRULY VALUED IN HEAVEN

THE TRINITY

God, Jesus and the Holy Spirit . . .

They say that a trinity exists between God and Jesus and the Holy Spirit. These beings are in unison and in harmony and completely one. We have no concept of this, we only have examples of it within our society and you must know where to look.

We all know to drive on the right side of the road. We all know if we stick our hand in a fire we will get burned so do not do it. We all breathe. We all sleep. We eat. We are in harmony and unison within certain aspects of our existence. A person could spend a lifetime wondering and pondering the relationship of the trinity.

There is also a different trinity that exists that no one knows about. It is the trinity that we share or should share with each other. We can have a relationship of trinity with each other if we wanted to have one but we must first know about it and be taught about it. I was taught about it but have not mastered it yet I only understand the concept.

In our world 3 different people given the same choice will make 3 different choices. One person will steal. One person might contemplate it and not do it. One person will not consider it as an option or contemplate it. This is an example of non-harmony and non-unison.

3 spirits in heaven would all make the same choice. They would choose not to steal. You can bet on it every time. They are in harmony and in unison with God and have been taught a complete knowledge about existence and true life. They would choose not to steal so they would not defile their state of being and state of harmony with the everlasting and the eternal God.

On earth we must fight for this. We must fight everyday every step of our lives to resist theft and resist a lie and resist polluting our spirit.

There is also a different type of trinity that very few are aware of and that is a trinity of love that exists between 2 people that want to be one and close beyond physical understanding. It is a harmony of spirit and trust and selfless love. It is created with people and God. It all starts with the selfless love. 2 people that give themselves to each other completely and think of the other person first and think of themselves never (not last but never). Two people with God involved following the same spirit for life making the same choices given the same options will begin to create a trinity of a biblical dynamic but people do not know about so they never find it.

Instead of simply acknowledging that there is a trinity between those in heaven, seek to create your own between you and the ones that you love with God involved. Get involved with God and God will get involved with you. You being to feel a closeness and a kinship that will go beyond time and space and you will know that the other person when out on their own will face situations and you will know that they will be safe and make good choices. I have just learned about this concept myself so it is very difficult to describe but I am sure that I will try to create this with those around me.

The first step to this path is selfless behavior not self centered or selfish behavior. Before taking a path one must first study all aspects of it before participating.

Chapter 8

God led me to suicide not the Devil

Why do I say that God led me to do this and not the Devil? . . .

When I tell people that God led me into suicide or to be more precise God led me through suicide and brought me to a better state of being on the other side of death. People never seem to give God the credit and the Glory that is due to God. God is the inventor of death. God is the builder of time and space. God is my creator. From this point of view we have no rights that are our own. God simply allows us to be, no matter what we do to ourselves. God is my creator and can do as God pleases with me. Few people understand this. Fewer still allow God to act upon this in their lives. God has led many people to contradict the commandments. For instance why would God give the Jewish people the law and the commandments and then ask Abraham to kill his own son. Why did Abraham not rebuke the spirit that asked him to kill his own son? I can tell you the answer to this. It is simple. When God decides to reveal himself to you and ask you to do something that is contradictory to the commandments or even common sense God lets you know that he is God asking you and leading you to do this. If God himself did not lead me through my suicide I don't know where my spirit would be right now. When God asks you to do something, you know that it is God.

The devil was there as well, constantly trying to corrupt the situation. The devil constantly tried to rob me of my faith and trust in God. God is my creator and the creator of death. When you step out of your limited faith and truly spiritually trust beyond what you think you know then you begin to see yourself and God. I trusted God beyond all physical and mental limitations. I trusted that God knows and can do everything and I can do nothing. The devil knew what God planned to do for me. I did not. The devil knew what was in store for me that is why the devil kept trying to stop me from doing this. If I did not keep my promise to God then God could not have performed his miracle of salvation for me. The devil does not want us to have any type of interaction with God whatsoever. The devil certainly does not want someone to receive the gift of the salvation of Jesus and then start wandering the earth telling others about what was done for me. The devil was completely satisfied with me as a pure hearted sinner, the devil certainly did not want me seeking my death and salvation or die and search for Jesus, trusting in Jesus for him to find me and come to me. God has made me a threat to the existence of evil itself.

God is making me into something and I would help God continue this and work with God to finish his work in me.

There are other times in the bible when God asked people, his faithful people, to do something contradictory to life. God has asked his faithful to wipe out entire villages and entire peoples including women and children. Why did those people not question God saying, God it cant be you asking me to do this, you are the God of life. Why would God ask Saul and Samuel to wipe out a small town or village to the last person including women and children? When God asks these things God also reveals himself so that you know that it is God asking you to do these things and no one else. God also showed me the devil and allowed me to see how the devil kept trying to corrupt the situation and keep this from coming into existence. Study your bible. You will find God to be a God of wrath and a God of love. I can however clear this up some. God is not a God of wrath. God is a God of righteousness. Good and evil cant exist inside the same being or person. This is the great conflict that resides inside us all until the time of our personal death. There are no sinners in heaven. The old person that you are must be completely destroyed before you can enter heaven. The old person that you are must be completely destroyed then completely recreated by God into the image of God through the death and resurrection of Jesus. I know this because I lived it out while here on earth. This is the secret that the devil does not want on earth.

These are the end times. This being done to me is the beginning of the end for the reign of evil on earth. God is coming soon. Evil will be erased from this planet as if it never were here. We are all destined to be recreated and leave this sin filled flesh behind. There are no sinners in heaven. People don't run around there in a state of confusion asking for constant forgiveness and acting like sin does not exist.

Think about what my story of what God did to me will affect others. What God did to me will cause others to have more faith in God not less faith in God. This is why the devil did not want this. There comes a point in knowing the truth and God where the devil cannot steal that which God gives to your heart. The Devil does not want this story of mine and Gods presence in my life to be known to those people that are willing to believe what I say here to be the truth. The Devil does not want people to believe that God did this for me. The devil does not want the faith of others fortified against the devil. This story may build clarity in others not confusion. All I can say is this: I did do what I say I did and God must have done what God did. You may believe these things. You may believe that God has forgiven us of our worst most horrific sins, even the ones that we believe are unforgivable such as suicide. God does not play favorites. I am no one special. What God does for one he will do for others also. Forgiveness is a gift waiting for all to receive. God wants the worst of the worst to repent so that they may be saved and receive. I'm not saying to you commit suicide, don't miss interpret what I am saying to you. Think hard and you will see what I'm saying to you. I committed suicide and I'm telling you NOT to commit suicide but at the same time I am telling you that what God did for me he will do for others. So what did God do for me? I was forgiven. I was forgiven of my sins. I was forgiven of my sins and in this forgiveness God was allowed back into my heart. You don't need to die to be forgiven in this life. I took it to the extreme but this is not needed in others for them to receive forgiveness. Stop the destruction in your life before it starts. Think about what God is saying to you and let it become clear. Study your bible harder now than ever before.

POINTS OF INTEREST TO PONDER

Biblical facts:

God led Jesus to die and allowed and wanted him to be crucified.

The Devil tried to stop Jesus by using his follower Peter to stop him from being crucified and Jesus called him Satan, "get behind me Satan . . ."

God led Jesus to do what he did and explained what was going to happen well in advance of the crucifixion. Jesus told others this.

CHAPTER 9

DREAM JOURNAL, STRANGE THINGS . . . .

Nov, 18,2005
Dream Journal

Dear God and Savior and Spirit,

I will write in detail all the dreams that I feel and know are Dreams given to me
as you give them.

11/19/05

My first dream to describe is unbelievable. I think that my hardest problem that
I'm going to have is actually finding the words to describe these events to other
people that do not experience these things. These writings may help others with
the same experiences brought about by the Living God.

I fell asleep praying and writing in my prayer journal about the Holy Spirit finding
me and coming into my body to dwell as the Holy Spirit went to dwell with
Jesus. God began to speak to me and quietly asked me if I am ready for God to
come to me in that manner. My response is the manner in which I am changing
and becoming closer to what God wants, my reply was simple I said that at this
point in my life and at this time I am as willing and ready and as able as the
experiences that have been with have made me. I am as ready as you have made
me at this point God and no further along than that. I fell asleep pondering this
simple fact. God is the God of the living and the True Living God in the land of
the living; we are in the land of the dead in spirit or dormant in spirit.

The dream and my dreams:

My dreams these days are different since my death and being risen. My consciousness is awake and aware while I sleep. It is as if I am still awake and aware even while I am asleep, this is the best way to describe it. I was lying on my back in a bed. My sister had come into the room; she was younger and happier in appearance. It felt like a visitation from my true sister from the land of the living, being Gods realm. It was my real sister in appearance but from the inside out she was completely different, with love and light from the inside out. She sat down on another bed across the room and said. I know where Jesus is. I said where and she said there and pointed at me. At that moment Jesus, For lack of a better word either possessed me or entered my body or temple of my body as it is referred to in the bible. When that moment happened things became very, very real and I was in the land of the living God. Jesus was truly in my body and making himself aware to me in a different way, the Trinity, God, Son and Holy Spirit was awakening. The sound was strange, I heard a ringing or musical note, the light that came from me from the inside out and has a consciousness of its own and the pure power of that type of living energy electrified my body. This experience was not manufactured like other dreams. My imagination is not that vivid. This was a real spiritual experience of spiritual awakening while my body slept. The light that came out of me from the inside out was the light and power of God the Trinity. I believe that this dream is a foretelling of events to come and if God does decide to baptize me in the Holy spirit in the same manner as Jesus was, all the people that I meet are about to be very abruptly changed. Someone recently told me that Moses had this light shine from him from being in the presence of God and people asked him to wear a veil. I will do God no disservice by letting others force me to diminish God. People will need to either leave or allow themselves to be lifted up by the Holy Spirit that is coming forth. This dream has taught me one thing, if that state of consciousness that God allowed me to experience for a few minutes is our true state of consciousness then we truly are dead and dormant in the spirit. For a moment I was the being that God intends to create in me and if this state of Living Light remains in me then all who meet and see me are about to be changed for the better in all ways.

My prayer now, please God continue to let me experience, learn and listen and simply write what you do with me and I will strain to find the words to describe you. God please continue. Dearest Holy Spirit, my heart is waiting to be your new home if you would come from the land of the living to dwell in this land of the dead you may have my heart as your dwelling place of safety and refuge from all the evil that exists in other people and all the evil of Satan in this world. God has shown me many things about those that dwell in heaven and if you are as it is described to me the you will need a completely willing heart and body to take refuge here from what is in this world.

This next dream that I am describing is very significant but occurred many years ago. It happened to me one night during the late 90's. It was when another country was testing nuclear weapons under ground, if I remember correctly it was Korea.

I feel asleep pondering what it must have been like for the people of Hiroshima and Nagasaki when the bombs fell in WWII. I was asking God what it was like to be one of those people. God allowed me to experience what it was like to be near a nuclear explosion in a dream. When you experience a dream that is from God the dream is more real than this life itself or any dream you have without God. God lets you know it is from him. As the nuclear explosion hit in my dream I was very abruptly woken up and when I woke up a pure form of the power of God filled the house. I woke my girlfriend up and she watched me run around the house frantic yelling that God in Coming, God is coming. Pure living energy with an ability of complete self control because my girlfriend could not feel it, I was the only one that was allowed to experience the sensation of Gods presence. For some unknown reason to me God has been communicating things to me my entire life and is doing this on a systematic basis throughout my life.

Let me write a brief outline.

1. I was 18-19 and my girlfriend hurt her hand and Jesus visited us that night while we waited and healed her hand.
2. Near the end of October a few weeks later, God/ Jesus allowed me to experience crucifixion. God crucified me in a church courtyard.
3. I experienced a real spiritual change fundamentally; the question of Gods existence was answered for me.
4. Then I wandered around for months asking to pray and see people healed. I once asked God to heal a professed atheist, she hand some type of cold/flu. God whispered to me saying touch her and say be healed. I did and when I saw her again she said the strangest thing happened to her, one minute she was sitting on the couch sneezing and aching and then it was just gone as if it was never there.
5. Then the darkness came and I fell. I started asking questions to God and the real pain of the cross began to press down on me. It was as if my soul were ripped in half and ripped open. Sadness came into and seemed that it would never leave. I experienced the most fundamental sadness of the cross, abandonment. I kept asking God why did God forget about

me or forsake me. God gave me no reply. I decided to turn my back on the whole situation and God. I fell from grace. Then I began to seek my own will and pursue all manner of everything.

6. 15 years went by and the empty hole inside me just kept getting bigger no matter how much money or sex or seduction that I poured into it. There is a hole inside us that only God can fill and fit into to satisfy us.

7. At this point it hurt tremendously to even think of going into a church or even watch the shinny happy people in Christ. Others get fun and joy and I was made to suffer for Jesus by being put on the cross with him. Bearing the cross of our savior is no joke to say the least.

8. All that time God still gave me dreams and talked to me and showed me things inside other people.

9. When going against Gods will most of the things that God says to you are mostly don't do that.

10. Then I got married and decided to die, was led into my death by God and given my life back by God.

This is the basic outline to be added to as details are remembered.

12/7/2005

It was a dream like any other, nothing special. Then it happened. I was in the tunnel. I was in the tunnel and traveling down the tunnel and I could see and feel the living light at the end of the tunnel. I knew this dream was real. I knew the living light that I was seeing and experiencing was real. I was not allowed to leave the tunnel. I never made it to the end to come out the other side. I could feel the light at the end of the tunnel and it was so strong and so penetrating that it woke me up. This dream lasted only for a moment but it felt very significant to me.

12/12/2005

These next 2 dreams happened back to back one day after the other. I was attacked the first night. Something evil either, the Devil or something from the devil settled upon me while I slept and basically held me down, growled at me tried to taint my spirit in some way and caused the wounds of Christ in my hands to start bleeding. This evil being also sat on top of me for several moments and then caused some type of paralysis to occur in my arms. I was being held down and not let move. I was being assaulted by some strange being of evil that just decided to run up and start beating on someone. This seems to be a desperate act to me, the devil seldom chooses a frontal brutal assault unless the devil is really frustrated with someone and cant corrupt them.

The second day and the second dream was a dream about a great woman that has the appearance of a whore. She spoke in the dream to me and at me and referred to Satan in the dream as "lord Satan" I did not really understand the rest of the words in her sentences because they were spoken softly but she did refer to Satan in the dream as "lord Satan". She was very pale and her clothes were strangely colored. Her hair extended outward from her head her face was pale and white in complexion with dark makeup around her lips. We were inside what looked like a cave and there was something like sand on the ground and the walls were jagged rocks. On the ground in front of her was a dragon, she seemed to worship this item and out of its mouth was a long tongue that was purple in color and the dragon was brightly colored. The dragon was lying down as in a sleeping position and did not move. This dream was a real first to me because I have never in my life even in movies or TV heard Satan referred to as "Lord" It seems even more odd to me that these words would be spoken to me in a dream. It is very seldom that I dream of evil in this manner. Most dreams I have are either of the future, meaning my personal future and events that will happen in my personal life or dreams about God and what God is in all Gods forms. These dreams mean something that is not yet known to me. They are however valid but their meaning is not yet apparent.

2/13/2006

Last night the light power enveloped me in a completely different manner. This time I maintained consciousness and was able to talk and speak. These images were very strange but after being in the light/power and being a part of the light/power the images were not as important as what I was finally able to do which was interact and speak. In this state of being which I am now while awake and conscious the light power is so overwhelming that it is very near the sensation of electrocution or being flooded with so much raw energy that it is impossible to move or speak. It is raw unimaginable pure light and power. At this point in my awareness I am not aware of the extent of the ability of this light /power I only know how it affects me on a singular personal level which is like being submerged in pure electricity but it does not kill it simply incapacitates. The Dream itself was very simple. For moments God and I had become ONE. I was aware of God and God was aware of me. This time, there have been others, but this time I was able to speak and think and see and move. I saw myself. My first thought was that God has made me into a beggar and I constantly beg God for spiritual things for all mankind. I was wearing brown robes, very plain and ordinary. I was not alone inside myself. I was part of a greater whole. The prayer that fell from my lips was repeated over and over again. "God give them love in their hearts straight from heaven." What does this statement mean? It means that I see what is absent from the hearts of all men. There is no love that is similar to the love that is in the hearts of those that live in heaven and all mankind needs this love in the center of their being.

Many observers in this dream surrounded me. They had a state of awareness that was outside the collective whole that I was inside with God but they were also part of God as well. They watched as I ACTED. In front of me stood a white column or pillar in the room and on top of this column were many candles perhaps seven in all I did not count perhaps more or less. What was significant was what the candles did. The candles were not lit but when I called Gods name or shouted to God the candles lit by themselves. One candle that was in the center of the group of candles was immediately consumed by a light blue flame. There was also a small statue near the group of candles. This statue seemed to represent evil. As I prayed to God asking for love in the hearts of all people the face on the statue changed and began to become more and more filled with hatred specifically for me. This hatred seemed to become filled with even more hatred as it realized that it could not harm me. As I spoke within this light/power my voice had taken on a different aspect. It was deeper and full, it was as if my spirit was speaking or the spirit within was speaking instead of the plain physical voice of vocal cords. I believe this phenomenon to be the true interpretation of the meaning of the scripture, speaking in other tongues. This dream continued into this reality and into this consciousness. I say this because when I had awoken from my dream, which was a gentle awakening, my voice was still different. I was lying there praying to God and continuing our conversation. I am still trying to figure out what it is that God is creating me into. What am I becoming after being in the hands of the creator and what is God making me into? I know that God creates us in his own image. The problem with this is that none of us know exactly what that image is. All the thoughts and ideas of God are basically wrong. WE, meaning all mankind, do not know God, some DO know God but these few are the ones that God isolates and reveals himself to in a very secret and complete way. I say this after seeing God for the first time and referencing this that I saw with what I know of the ideas of all mankind and what they perceive God to be. In the dream I prayed and maintained my awareness and ability to walk and talk and think inside this light/power and each time this power consumes me I become more accustomed to it and living inside it and I become more and more a part of it and the light /power becomes more a part of me. I am spiritually merging with whatever this is.

5/15/2006

Recently in a dream while I was awake, I saw the Holy Spirit descend on me and it did coincidentally look like a dove flying. It was so beautiful and quiet and soft and amazing. I also had a dream of a day of Pentecost. There was a great rushing wind and then the spirit of power fell on me and it was unbelievable.

I also saw a huge bolt of lightning hit the ground in a vision while praying.

6/25/2006

Last night was an amazing dream. I felt this light power again and it was in the room even after I was awake and the dream had left me. Here are the events in the dream. I was outside looking up at the night sky and as I was looking up into the night sky and there was some type of explosion. It was as if a star had exploded. Then what appeared to be some type of meteor shower from many different directions came into earth's atmosphere. The meteor shower glowed and the moon seemed to change color and there was a strange type of different light that came from the moon. The people that surrounded me in the dream seemed to believe that this was a sign that Jesus was returning soon. We all held hands in the dream and felt this. The moon was low in the sky and the explosion took place to the upper left of the moon. It was incredible to see. The earth lit up for a moment.

In this dream I was not told what anything was. It could have been a star exploding or it could have been a missile that was detonated in a very high orbit. There was a meteor shower directly after the explosion so it might have been a missile that was launched at a large meteor coming to earth and the fallout was the meteor shower. I do not know.

I only know that this dream had the same characteristics as the other ones, the white light power was present and was all around me to the point of terror. When this white power is on you it makes you full of terror if you cannot control yourself.

These dreams with the white power are different from the dreams that are visions of my life because the white power is not a predominant or not as powerful in presence. As I look back the dreams with the white light power are always about global events and things of this nature as if a being is present and showing me the world and not showing me myself.

Chapter 10

The testimonial of others . . . .

People that knew me before and after . . . .
Exerts from interactions with other people and Gods
involvement . . .

This is from a friend of mine that has a husband in a wheel chair.
She writes this about me . . . .

I knew something was different when I got an e-mail from Chris signed, "Love, CMK." I had known Chris for about nine years, and in all that time he'd never signed anything, "Love."

The e-mail was the first I'd heard from him in months. His wife had been away for about two months the last time I'd spoken to him on the phone. He sounded terrible, I think worse than I'd ever heard him sound. He just sounded broken and unhappy and hopeless. I lost touch with him after that conversation because his cell phone stopped working, and I had no other way to contact him except e-mail. He wasn't replying. Every so often, I'd send an e-mail on the off chance that he would check, but I didn't hear from him for months. Then, out of the blue, I got an e-mail about how he had a long story to tell me about God and Jesus that would change my perception about reality. And he signed it, "Love, CMK," so I knew something had happened.

In the next e-mail, Chris told me how he killed himself and God healed him and sent him back. It was quite a powerful story. He wrote about why he thought he was sent back and what God was like. He wrote pages and pages over the next couple of

105

weeks, all about God, Jesus and the Holy Spirit, which was very unusual. In all the time I'd known him, I can't remember him talking about God, and now that was all he was writing about. The way he was writing sounded exactly like Chris, but it wasn't like him at all to be talking about God. It was a very profound change.

It was the same when I saw him a few weeks later. Outwardly, he looked the same, although he'd lost some weight. What was different from the last time I saw him was that he seemed happy and peaceful. When other people were around, he talked about ordinary things, but when we were alone, after some small talk, he told me again about what happened to him the night he killed himself and what had happened since then. He also told me some stories from his past that I had not heard before, like when he was crucified. He wanted us to go to a nearby church and talk, which we did. Chris felt moved to confess something to God, and he wanted me to be a witness. He held my hand and spoke aloud briefly to God. Then we talked for a while longer, mostly about God and prayer and faith. He encouraged me to pray every day.

We spent six or seven hours together that night, and about half of that time was spent talking about faith. Throughout the night, I kept thinking how odd it was. Chris looked the same, and he sounded the same, but the things he was talking about were so radically different from what we normally discussed. I kept looking over at him to make sure he was the same person. All these things kept flowing out of him, quite naturally, but I'd never heard him say anything like it before in the nine years that I'd known him. He was different, but not in a "crazy" or bad way. He seemed much happier than usual, although, strangely, not satisfied. Chris essentially said that all he wants to do now is help people and serve God, but he's impatient to go back to God. He doesn't really want to be here anymore, but he knows now that he can't do anything to hurry that along, because God will only take him back when he's ready.

I have begun to think about things in terms of the "New Chris" and the "Old Chris." The "Old Chris" never talked about God with me, but the "New Chris" is eager to discuss his faith with certain people. (I don't think he goes up to just anyone and starts talking about God.) The "Old Chris" was not as concerned with helping people, although he did try to take care of those who were close to him. And he was much more concerned with attaining his own goals of a house and land and money for himself and his family.

The "New Chris" doesn't seem to want anything for himself; he only wants to help people and serve God. The "Old Chris" offered to build me and my disabled husband a wheelchair-friendly house, which was a very generous offer.

So generous, in fact, that we never actually did it. My husband and I were not in a position to commit to a house. But the "New Chris" made a much more realistic offer; he said he would come help me take care of my husband. That will be quite an undertaking, since we live on the other side of the country in a one-bedroom apartment with no couch. He'll have to sleep on the floor. But he wrote, and these words stuck in my mind because I never heard him say anything like it before, "I'll sleep on the floor if I have to. Your needs are greater than mine." That's definitely the "New Chris" talking.

Hearing about Chris' experiences has made me think about my own faith a lot recently. I do pray more than I used to, and I went to Mass yesterday for the first time in years. I don't know what will happen, but the "New Chris" has had at least a short-term positive effect on my life, and I'm grateful for it.

FROM CHRIS KING . . .

As a Child of God I need to reassert a few things when reading this. The first thing that come to mind for me when reading this is the concept of the old me and the new me. The bible refers to this as the old man crucified, and the new resurrected child in God through Jesus. What I need to point out here is that all these changes that occurred in me, I did not do. God performed these changes in me by simply teaching me a few simple rights from wrongs that are real in the spiritual world and not the physical world. Any change or differences in my spirituality, and me, God must get all credit and glory. It was Gods glory that gave me the few changes that exist in my heart and it was a hard price to pay for these few things. God is not done with me, I have a long way to go and I believe that this is just the beginning of a new and very different life for me. I hope to add more to this list of testimony to God before this book is published. This list of testimony is not about me and the changes in me, it is about the influence that the living God has had on me and the changes that the living God has made in me after interacting with me in my life on earth.

During my 18th to 19th year, 1986/87
THE 20DOLLAR BILL AND THE HOMELESS MAN

From the book of Isaiah 42:16
And I will lead the blind by a way that they do not know,
In paths they do not know, I will guide them.
I will make darkness into light before them.

***

I had/have a friend named Lawrence. We knew each other in high school. God drew me close through my Stigmata experience in the courtyard that night and Lawrence knew me as a practicing Christian. One night Lawrence and I went to Georgetown in DC and we encountered a homeless man begging. I had a 20-dollar bill in my pocket and proceeded to give the man that money and just kept walking. Lawrence was not upset but perplexed and asked why did I do that, he could have used that 20. My reply was simple; I could have used it also but that man needed it more. Lawrence bought us food that night since I just gave all my money away.

Now we fast forward to 2005. When I gave that money to that man that night, Jesus was my motivation for giving, not the needs of the homeless man or for the purpose of making myself look good or giving Lawrence a big question mark towards my actions. When you act faithfully to Jesus in all situations it gives a different meaning to your life. Lawrence was not asking me why did Chris give that money away, Lawrence was in reality asking in a spiritual way unknown to Lawrence, "Why did you Jesus have Chris King give that 20 dollar bill away?"

Today is the year 2005 and Lawrence now knows why. I met Lawrence again on Sun, Nov 20th 2005 and found him wandering out of church as I was sitting in the back row. I have not been in that church for 15 years and found it to be a strange coincidence. There is no such thing as a coincidence with God in your life and leading you. I once ministered to the homeless from that church many years ago and returned there simply out of sentiment. Lawrence said that he was just thinking about me a few days earlier and all our encounters and God had planted the image of that $20 in my mind a few days earlier as well. Lawrence knows that meaning of the 20-dollar bill because Jesus has been leading Lawrence through his life in manners known and unknown to him. Today Lawrence is in charge of a halfway house for recovering drug addicts and homeless. He is actually living out what I once fantasized for myself to do, but never had the opportunity. He is in charge of 2 thrift stores that help the needy and the poor. Jesus answered Lawrence's question by having him live out the answer. Lawrence is now that answer to other peoples prayers. Larry now has what others need and is giving freely as others give to him.

I look back at all the time we spent and interacted together in life and I see Jesus being involved in every situation. Jesus has had a hand in our involvement together. It is in fact a beautiful thing to look back on and a beautiful thing to look forward to ahead. I pray that God watch over Lawrence as vigorously as God watches over me.

A CHAPTER CALLED LESLEY....

3/28/2006

Above is today's date and this is a new addition to the book that I am writing and as I have said in other places in this book, this is a book that is written by someone that is experiencing a mystery that is alive and changes on a daily basis. That mystery is God and how God influences our lives and influences others through our life. As of the date above I am working in a fast food restaurant and have no financial prospect what so ever. This reminds me of the Franciscan monks vow of deliberate poverty and their belief in the poverty of Jesus while on earth. I also finding myself living and breathing the scripture "not for profit servant", this term, God is giving literal meaning in my life and is taking the not for profit servant just a little to far but I can handle it.

I work at a fast food restaurant and a woman that works there with me named Lesley was evicted from her home by her boyfriend. Lesley has two children the oldest is 6. Lesley started sleeping in her car with the kids for a few days and took her family to a homeless shelter and wandered around town looking for someplace to live.

Last night she slept on my couch. This is the extent of my involvement. When she woke up this morning **I thanked her** for staying in my house and she could not figure out why I would say thank you for a favor that I did for her. This book is about God not me. God has been telling me things about Lesley and I have been passing on the information. God has been showing me her life and I have been passing this information back to her. Later on I will sit her down and ask her to tell all the things that I said to her that I could not possibly have know because she did not tell me. Lesley is a suicide victim although she never succeeded in completing the act of suicide. There have been numerous times in her life when she attempted and tried and even thought about or obsessed about her own death. God showed this to me. I told her and it seemed to frighten her somewhat.

As of today Lesley does not know about my story and as of today and the past few weeks she is forbidden to know about me and what happened to me. God is calling her and using me and my relationship with God to help Lesley be set free from certain things.

I have taken Lesley to church twice and I personally saw God speaking to her heart and she began to cry each time. God speaking to her was not an audible voice like

I hear God, it was more of an instinctive spiritual deep level that words can't bring into focus. She knew and she felt it and she responded. Lesley made the comment while we were at church that she believes that God has specifically put me in her life on these very days for a reason that serves God will and God love and purpose. In the past week I have watched Lesley be tempted and tormented by many things. Her boyfriend that threw her out forbid her to go to church and then asked her why did she not invite him to go. Since she has been gone for a few days the boyfriend is now coming to the restaurant and is looking for her, no doubt to give a difficult time. He is certainly not there to repent. I am in Lesley's life because she is ready to repent and break that life long pattern of self-abuse and self-torture that she has lived through. I can only say that at this point I will do my best and most humblest of things to serve God. I will repeat all that God speaks to me and deny no information to her about God or herself. I will give what I can where I can and do what I can as God directs me. Sometimes I need to back away and let God take over and do what God needs to do. That is the difficult thing to realize. This is not about me anymore. It is about the world and all those that I encounter. She needs information that I have and needs the being that I know and wish to serve. I will not tell her about what I did until that latest of moments and never if it is possible. I do not want what I did interfering with her relationship with God.

God wishes to help in many ways and I will tell a few of these things. Jesus gives sight to the blind. Lesley is not physically blind; she is spiritually blind as we all are. God wishes for her to see her actions and the outcome and the torment or the pleasure that results from what we do.

Jesus gives the lame the ability to walk. Lesley is not lame but does not have the ability to walk through the torment of looking at herself and seeing herself as God sees her so Jesus will give her legs to walk through things also.

What is yet to come, I do not know. Tomorrow she may fall away or be on my couch for another night. I do not know. I met the moment as it comes. I repeat what I hear. That is all I can do. I told her thank you for sleeping on my couch because it is a chance for me to pass on the spiritual wealth that was given to me while I was in WVA planning my suicide. There were people that let me stay with them and gave me a couch when I needed it so I pass this on to honor what was given to me. I spent the night praying, thanking God for this moment and telling God how this moment does not belong to me, it belongs to those that provided for me, when I needed a couch to sleep on. So I pass on what was done for me. Lesley does not know about what happened to me. I prefer my story to remain a mystery for now. I want her and everyone to know God, not me. I want her and everyone to know what God does for us not what I did for her.

The first place that God takes us is repentance and in repentance we find a form of death. Will she survive the type of repentance that the living God will place on her? It is up to her and to God. So let me give you some coincidental quotes and conversations between her and I

Lesley asked, "When will it all change?" I replied, "When you change." Lesley replied, "OUCH."

At church she made a statement. "God has put me(Chris) in her life right now,"

I did not reply to that because thoughts of my own resurrection came to mind so I simply remained quiet. If God had allowed me to die and not healed me and resurrected me then I would not have been sitting there so it is absolutely true that God put me there although I decided to keep it all a secret for now.

I told Lesley, "God tells me things, Chris knows stuff," referring to myself in the third person.

Lesley said, "Tell me something about me you know." I told her "You feel cursed and that God has cursed you," This statement gave her a moment of pause. The next day she came up to me and asked me "How did you know that I feel cursed and have felt cursed most of my life?"

I didn't but God does. God can talk to people.

Sunday before church we talked and I told her, "God has told me more things about you."

She said, "What, tell me." I asked her, "How many times have you attempted suicide?" Already knowing the answer is many times and obsessed about it even more.

She simply started talking then turned to tears as the images of all those times came into her mind. I know this because God allowed me to watch as the memories came back into her consciousness.

Lesley is still being tempted and when she leaves me I know she goes to meet the devil himself. Evil does not want people returning to God. She asked me the other day about prostitution and would God get mad at her if she started doing something like that? My reply was candid. I said that Jesus told the prostitutes their sins were forgiven, sin no more, not go turn a few more tricks. That's just a little Jesus humor. God does have a wonderful sense of humor although I don't know how often people get to enjoy it.

I will write more entries later and date each one; this might turn out to be a most interesting chapter. I will ask Lesley if she will be interested in writing in my book but I will call it a prayer journal and not tell her what it is really about so everything remains authentic and a real mystery to her.

The first step in returning to God is repentance. To repent is an action. In order to repent we must first become self-aware and know all that we do and all that we are so that we may turn away from it. Turning away from our old self is where death occurs. As we repent we must commit ourselves to murder that which we were so that we may never return to that state of being. This is the beginning of the mystery of repentance. It is deeper than these few words here can ever describe.

3/29/2006

The chapter called Lesley . . .

Its about 11pm and I was sitting here chatting with Lesley and asked her to tell me or describe some of the things that I told her about herself that I could not have possibly known.

Things Chris said that Chris could not have possibly known:

1: Chris knew that my suicides were while being married or during the times of marriage in my life. Lesley has been married 4 times.
2: Chris told Lesley that she felt cursed and it seemed to have stuck a nerve. She says that she has felt cursed ever since she was a little girl.
3: Chris said that God is coming back in your life now because you are willing to repent and have the potential for real repentance. She is tired of the cycle and is at the point of enough is enough and is willing to break the cycle.
4: Chris new that I am afraid to be alone in my life without the presence of a man to validate my existence

So as I sit here she just left the room. I find myself asking God or them, I refer to God as them, others like to use the word trinity I us "them", I find myself asking God what I could relay that might be of assistance to her and it is being shared with me that now is a time for her to simplify her life and continue to tear down the old life. Tear down the old patterns of self-hate and self-loathing and strip her "self" clean. I have not mentioned this concept to her and my greatest problem is simply communicating the concepts and ideas properly so that the course of action can be best understood. Now is the time for her to dig inside herself and find the root of the problems and start to see the nature of the mistakes that were made and how they were made. This must be done with Gods assistance and help and then God must be asked to help break the cycle. When we talk again I will tell her these things and see how she reacts. It is a time to simplify her life and not complicate problems more by turning to drugs or sex or habit/dead-end relationships while God is deliberately trying to help. Now is the time to let God show you things about yourself, repent, turn away from doing these things again and then allow God to heal you inside and then after a certain amount of time go and look for a relationship after educating yourself on how to get and keep and maintain real love that lasts and is not on a time limit or cycle of habitual behavior that always ends up in violence or divorce and hatred.

3/30/2006

Tonight Lesley and I discussed many things. I told her about the path. The path is a path of self-discovery and knowledge that God likes to lead people through. The path is a path that must be traveled with Jesus, which is why he called himself the Way, he is the Way back to God.

I told Lesley about herself again tonight, She is self-hating and self-loathing and has no sense of self-value or self worth. We talked in the parking lot of the restaurant for a short time. The first step is to repent. I told her it was going to be painful but a good kind of pain, not a bad type of pain.

4/3/2006
10:00pm

Tonight is the first night that Lesley and her 2 children will be staying here together. I find this situation almost identical to what happened to me in October of 2005. My son and I were in the same situation except we had a home to go to but at the time I could not bring myself to occupy the little house on my property because of haunting memories of all the things that my wife and I had done together. Her presence was too strong there and I could not take it without her company. You never realize how much we care for someone until they are gone. You also never really understand what you do until God really shows you yourself.

Tonight is the first night that her whole family will be here and it seems nice to share the little that I have at this point in my life. A simple couch at just the right moment can go a long way. Fortunately the couch folds out into a bed. I slept on this couch many times as a child and it seems nice to help others with it. I find it eerie and also a bit spooky at times when God uses me in peoples lives in this manner to put me in precisely the exact right moment at exactly the right time. It has been written in scripture that God is never late or early but exactly on time.

So here I am, sharing a couch and breakfast and sending them on their way into another day tomorrow morning. I think that I might make waffles, I just bought a new waffle iron and it should be fitting that I use it to feed these children. Once again I have a chance to repay a debt to all the people that gave me a couch to sleep on when I needed it so I pay it forward as the saying goes. Tonight I will ask Lesley if she has seen or heard anything strange with God and has God interacted with her in her life. It finally came to mind specifically what God wants to do. Lesley must be convicted of her sins and God wishes to do this. It is where God always starts with anyone. We must be convicted of sin so that we may understand what we are so that we can repent and turn away. It is obvious to me that we do not even have the capacity to understand what we are. I will speak to Lesley about this later and ask her for permission for God to convict her of her sins. I find synchronicity in this, being convicted of her sins because when I was on that couch in a friend's house last year I was being convicted of my sins, it was not pleasant in the least. We will see how she does. Will she be able to have the courage to simply stand and look at her self and take responsibility for what she has done to herself in her life or will she run away? Time will tell.

4/4/2006

It's late and I have just spent a great deal of time talking with Lesley and it seems that this story of hers has just became more interesting. She has just confided in me many different things about her past, many traumas and pains. The most interesting is that she also has died at least once perhaps 2 times but at least once for certain confirmed by her doctor. She died while giving birth to her son. This adds a completely different dynamic to the relationship between myself and God and her. It is obvious to me that she is in my life to give things to me as well as receive things from God and myself. As a person of God or child of God all I can do is simply commit myself to relay information, either what I see or what God tells me specifically. This is getting interesting. I wonder where it leads. I wonder when God is going to be seen and if we will be able to allow God to act?

4/6/2006

Last night I took Lesley to another church and introduced her to some real good people. We will go back on Sunday morning.

List of what is going on inside her:

There is a Self-hatred and desire for self-destruction; she seeks this treatment from others and herself

Cannot be alone with herself; she needs a man to validate her existence

Emotions are out of control; she has no control over her emotions, the things that should bother her do not and the things that bother her are trivial.

Ability to make a constructive choice in a bad situation is not there

Children act as a catalyst to provoke negative conduct in her and her children

Positive things:

Searching and looking for help

Deciding a different path than suicide

A strong urge to repent

Her desire to break the chain may be stronger than her desire to keep the chain

Things to do:

Make a commitment to yourself to help yourself get what you need

The truth is you do not want to die

The truth is that you want to live and find life

Pray everyday and do the opposite of what is on the bad list of things about you

Don't forget that God knows all the bad things about you and still chooses to love you

Pray every day and deliberately make time to pray and to sit and simply listen for the voice of God

Read and study the bible and truly try to understand as the word applies to the spirit of you, the bible is also about you, not just God

Before you can change yourself and your state of being such as pain or torment you must first understand what you are so you need to isolate and study what you are so that you can change.

Exercise your free will over yourself this is the only place that your free
will has real power, over yourself. If you can ruin your life then
you can repair your life.

Make choices that simplify your life not complicate it

Make choices that close the potential for disaster not open up the
possibility for disaster such as loaning things to people or getting
involved in bad situations

Stop the DRAMA, stop causing the drama, stop being the drama stop
participating in the drama, DRAMA QUEEN Learn what drama
is and then you can stop participating

Stop allowing life's daily situation to manipulate your emotional state
of being

Stop getting manipulated into arguments that take away the few things
that you have now

4/11/2006

Lesley has seemed to have moved on and has found a place to stay with the
children. I do not know how stable it is and where exactly she is but she makes
her own choices and lives them out, as we all must do. The last time I saw her it
seemed that God might have been leading her into a place of self-discovery. I do
not know. I only try and repeat what I hear and pass the word to others standing
next to me. This is my promise to God and those around me. My path to my life
is a different road than hers and I must go into my tomorrow as well.

4/25/2006
LESLEY AND JEFF . . . .
THE STORY GETS MORE INTERESTING . . .
GOD STEPS IN AND REVEALS HIMSELF
AND REVEALS JEFF TO HIMSELF

I don't know if you are enjoying reading this book, I am enjoying living it out,
sometimes, other times its very boring. Things have just become so completely
interesting and mysterious with the relationship of Lesley and Jeff. Jeff is the man
that originally put Lesley out and caused her to live on her own in the car. They
have gotten back together, their time apart has given them a chance to realize
they really care for each other and they seem to be getting determined to make
their relationship come together.

This however is not the interesting part. This next part that I am about to tell
you is either going to make a real believer out of you or a complete skeptic. I have

never met Jeff. I had never laid eyes on him until this date listed here. As I have said to people before, God talks to me. I hear and see and feel Gods voice talking to me. I made a promise to Lesley and also to Jeff that if God tells me something I will tell you both without hesitation or reservation. One day recently Lesley came to me at work and said that she needed to tell me something. I stepped to the side and said what? She said that Jeff seen the devil last night and it scared him so bad that he turned pale in front of her eyes. I said excuse me? Tell me that again. Lesley said that Jeff seen the devil standing in the doorway and the devil was motioning his arm at Jeff to come with him out the door. Lesley ran up and closed the door. Jeff was wide-awake and had not been drinking and very frankly could not believe what he was seeing. I said Ok Lesley, I need to meet with Jeff and talk to him.

God is one tricky God I must tell you and reveals Himself in so many mysterious ways and to use a cliché, God does not like to let the cat out of the bag too soon. God never told me that I was going to be involved in helping restore or try to restore the relationship of God and Lesley and the salvation of Lesley and God never told me that I was to help restore the relationship of God and Jeff and the salvation of Jeff. It is clear to me that this is what God is using me for, an instrument of restoration and a catalyst to return people to their path or salvation through Jesus.

I met with Jeff today and we had one of the most interesting conversations I have ever had. God began revealing things to me about Jeff's past life. God began to show me Jeff's past and several people that Jeff had affected in life.

Lesley was trying to explain to Jeff that God talks to me because she had told him about how I knew things about her that had been told to me by God. I told Lesley to go home and tell him my story and what had happened to me, about dying and meeting God and being sent back. I told her to tell him because she was telling me that he has become suicidal. So in that span of time, the devil came calling and literally stood outside Jeff's door and allowed Jeff to see him and even motioned, come with me. I asked Jeff if the devil spoke and he said no, just motioned. Then we really started talking.

So I am at a loss as to how to explain so much information that took place in so short a time. We talked a great deal about some very important issues that concern everyone, meaning salvation and heaven and hell.

So let's try to start at the beginning, I sat there quietly in the car, in the back seat riding with Lesley and Jeff on the way to my house to sit and talk. As I sat there God began to reveal things to me. Jeff is a Vietnam vet and struggles with very deep feelings of guilt about things that happened in Vietnam regarding killing people and issues of that nature. I began to ask God questions, is this man a cold hearted murdered or what? God what is he; show me what ever it is that You would like to show me. As I stood there and looked at him God showed me that he is a hero, which is the word that came to mind and that is the word that I used when I said it quietly to Lesley. This man is no murderer; he is a hero and a very valiant and brave spirit and valiant soul. God showed me that God loves Jeff.

You will know why I say Jeff is a hero and valiant after these next few paragraphs.

God then revealed to me that Jeff regretted the killing that he did during Vietnam and it torments him to this day that he has taken life from other men. God showed me that the battles he fought in were not about killing the enemy but it was about keeping yourself and your buddies next to you alive and there was one person that God showed me in particular that I later told Jeff about. As I sat there and stared at Jeff, God showed me heaven and earth and Jeff's life and the life of a spirit that is in heaven now. During his time in Vietnam, a man died in Jeff's arms. This was a man that Jeff ran after to rescue during a firefight. Jeff got up and ran through a hail of bullets to try and rescue another wounded solider. He was being shot at while running to the wounded soldier and was also being shot at while running away from the place where he picked up the wounded solider, trying to get him to safety. Imagine running with a man on your back while drawing fire. That's what happened, I don't really know how to explain; I'm not a combat veteran. The young man died in Jeff's arms at some point. God reveled to me that the young man that died has a tremendous love for Jeff and what Jeff did for that soldier that died that day in his arms. God showed me the love that waits for him in heaven from that dead soldier and it brought me to the point of tears in my heart.

Then the conversation became real interesting because I started tell Jeff all the things that God had told me. A man died in your arms one day; that person is in heaven now and thanks you for what you did and the gift and the personal sacrifice that you made for him. I was shown this. Jeff said to me that the things that I told him about himself without me knowing, since there was no way for me to know, was so accurate that it gave him chills right down to his spirit and soul. He knew there was no way for me to fake what I was saying to him. We then started talking about forgiveness. Will you allow yourself to forgive yourself? This was my basic question. The gift of forgiveness to others is something we are ready to give but we often forget to forgive ourselves and believe that we are also forgiven. I asked him point blank do you want to go to hell or do you believe that you are going to hell? He said that he needed to take some time to examine himself about that and figure out what he believes because he really does not know anymore.

God could have shown me anything he wanted to about Jeff and he showed me this story about the soldier dying in his arms. God chose that story to touch Jeff's heart and let him know that God is still there waiting for Jeff to accept his forgiveness and start living his life for Christ again and not for this world and stop living his life dictated by his sins.

They both have a difficult time ahead. It was interesting watching Jeff turn pale again as I told him about what was revealed to me about him. I cannot describe to you the complete joy and wonder that it is to have a true to life relationship with the real and true living God. I have never had such joy like this and you can only experience it by doing and living the bible, not by reading it. Jeff and Lesley and I are set to go to church this Sunday and I know that it will be wonderful. I look forward to it and am very happy to have them both as new friends, they are not just new friends they are new friends with God involved and Jesus involved and that makes the difference between life and death.

7/27/2006

Lesley and Jeff have been constantly at each other's throat since my last entry. They break up every few days and seem to keep going back for more. They have come to the conclusion that they need to change but do not know how. At Lesley's request, I called the local health department and found a number to free family and couple counseling. I gave her the number and she seemed happy to get it. She said she would call. We will see.

KYLENNE

4/8/2006

Today I finally told a friend of mine, KyLenne what really happened that day in West Virginia. Kylenne was the first person to see me after being returned or raised from the dead; I still do not know what to call it. She told me that she could tell there was something very different about me but did not know what it was. She described it as an inner peace that gave her the creeps. I have asked her to describe what she felt and saw exactly because Kylenne has also be dead and brought back again, she has her own very interesting story and I hope she chooses to speak about it. Kylenne died giving birth and met family members that had already passed away. I am asking her to describe the changes that she had seen

119

in me because these are changes that God personally made in me and things that happen as a result of interacting with the almighty God. Kylenne has some very interesting gifts as well and I hope she decides to write about those also.

Kylenne had seen me the morning that I had come back into town and spent the night fighting with God telling God how I was going to die and God spent the night telling me how I just was not. I don't know if you remember or not, I took 3 ounces of poison and it killed me and then I went out to my property and took the other 9 ounces which had no effect hence the evening of argument with God and me. As I have learned, when God decides something there is no arguing about it. To be honest I am glad God did send me back although I am still waiting to see if God will make me aware of a single concern that I had which was "God please do not send me back there alone without you!" I still am not sure what God has planned for me but sometimes it seems God is with me and sometimes life just seems normal like everyone else.

4/11/2006

Tonya under the bridge

Tonight is the first night that Tonya has stayed on the couch. We had a cookout today after I picked her up at the day labor office. Tonya and I made barbeque chicken and fixed hotdogs on the grill for the baby Christopher and the kids in the neighborhood. Tonya met a friend of hers that might turn out to be an interesting story; she died on the operating table and saw many things. This woman lives two doors down from me but I would have never known this if I did not decide to help Tonya in her particular situation. I will be writing about the neighbor at a later date, she promised to tell me her story also since we started talking about. I did not tell her mine; I just asked questions about what happened to her.

Tonya is the event at hand. I found Tonya living under a bridge in Florida, homeless and very ill. The way that we met is a very interesting story and I will try and detail it since God is directly involved.

Here is how the story goes; it's an interesting coincidence. I was busy painting a mural for a local restaurant owner who owns a restaurant that is directly next to a bridge that passes over the sound or inlet. I was standing out front talking with him trying to decide what to do with the mural and I asked him about the furniture that was under the bridge. He proceeded to tell me how people are living under there and the police will not chase them away and the owner of the place sounded as if these people living under the bridge were in his way almost as if they had no right to live or exist and no one ever fell on bad times and they just need to leave. I sat there listening to all this with many things going through my mind. There is a church in that same parking lot and I remembered how the plate gets passed around for people in other countries and all that good stuff while homeless people live directly in the parking lot. I pondered the irony of it and wondered if I was the only one that noticed this. I sat there holding the cross around my neck saying to myself and more directly to God, I remember asking God, I would specifically like to meet these people.

This is where the interesting part comes into focus. I was on the other side of town no where near the bridge and had no thought of encountering these people today and I decided to pull into a gas station and get some gas. It was around noon and I walked around the building to the other side of the gas station and walked to the door and at precisely the same moment those 3 people that I had seen living under the bridge came up and were timed in such a way that if you had seen it from a distance it looked like I had walked up and held the door open for them. This was a very noticeable action on Gods part since I had just asked God to allow me to meet them in a way that was not confrontational or a way that made me seem like some guy out to feed the homeless. As I held the door they walked in and as they walked out I held the door again, it just happened to be timed in this manner. Then I asked them if they needed anything and went home and put together a bag of clothes for the 2 guys and found some things for the woman, Tonya. She's the one on the couch right now. Then a few days later every time I would go looking for her I would ask God to let me find her and I did indeed happen to find her.

The second time we met was in the restaurant that is next to the bridge. I took her to buy her some Boost, it's a milkshake energy drink with vitamins and things. She was telling me that she was having trouble keeping food down and this might help. I took the last bit of money that I had and went and bought her two packs of Boost, strawberry flavor. I did not see her again for another few days and then she had told me that she was feeling much better and the drinks really helped. At that time I was busy cleaning out the closet and took her several bags of clothes. We spent some time talking and got to know each other.

I decided to ask her if she wanted to come and stay and get in off the streets for a while. She said to me that no less than 15 minutes after she had decided that she really wanted to get off the streets; I pulled up in the car and told her to get in. She said that it was strange that I would pull up and make this offer to her because she was just sitting there at the labor hall talking to someone about getting in off the streets.

Tonya is on the couch now; tonight belongs to her and God. I stole tonight for them both. I stole this night from all the evil people in the world that reject people and hurt people. I stole tonight for God and Tonya from the devil himself and all those that would disagree with what I am doing. I stole this night from evil so that some good could be done in the world because that is the kind of world that I want to live in.

I sit back and I wonder about scripture and all those people that say it and recite it but never seem to do it. I wonder if this is what Jesus meant by saying love thy neighbor, as you love yourself. Tonight I try to do, as you would tell me do and as you would have me do this night God. I stole tonight for you God. Tonight I do not read the bible, with God involved; I live and breathe the bible while God watches. I lay my free will at your feet God and hope to see your will be done before I leave this world again.

4/13/2006

Today I am sitting with Tonya and asking her general questions about this situation that she is in and the situation with my house and myself.

1: **Describe the campsite that you are living in at the bridge.**
4 tarps hanging over a wire, no tent, many blankets,

2: **Did you have problems with insects?**
No insect problems because of the cold but there was a problem with rodents and food left lying around.

3: **What is your daily routine?**
Wake up, wake up the other guys, go to labor hall, stay there, clean office, wander around town pushing a shopping cart filled with personal items that were deemed valuable.

4: **how long were you living on the street?**
From June 4th of 2005 to now.

5: **Is this the first time being homeless?**
Yes, I took to it like a duck to water.

6: **How old are you?**
46

7: **It has only been two days of sleeping on the couch, how do you like it?**
It's much better.

8: **What are some of your medical problems, chronic and superficial?**
Emphysema, chronic bronchitis, tracheotomy surgery done, pancreatitis,

9: **Do you feel that smoking is a major part of your problems?**
If I had not smoked it would not be so bad.

10: **It seems that you don't seem to care. How would you respond to this statement?**
I really don't care, if its time to go its time to go.

11: **What are you going to do to keep a roof over your head at the house of Mr. King?**
What ever, take care of the baby and the house.

12: **have you contemplated the fact that this might not work out with you staying here?**
I am prepared to go back to the way things were.

13: **What do you predict as the possible outcome of this situation of living here?**
We have no idea.

14: **What is your concept of my expectations with you being here?**
Do what you ask, take care of the baby, take care of the house and keep it clean and don't let a bad situation occur.

4/13/2006

It's the evening of the third day and Tonya has decided to go back to her camp. I explained my situation and what I expected and what I needed with the baby and going to work. She sat and answered these questions yet when it all came down to it she decided to stay out in the street tonight.

This reminds me of many different things in the bible and situations of God doing for people and people doing what ever with no regard for what is trying to be done for them.

I look back and wonder how it must have been like for Lazarus after he was raised from the other side. When Jesus healed him and called him back to this world it must have caused a great deal of trouble for the people in the temples and the priests. How can healing someone from the dead be trouble to those of this world? It is difficult to live like this is this state of flux between both worlds of this one and the next one.

Will she be on my couch tomorrow? Who knows? All I know is I tried to be faithful to the principles that God calls us to live by through out our lives such as love your neighbor as yourself. This is an every day thing that can take place anytime anywhere.

John, Soldier of God . . . 25 and on the streets . . .

I have recently met a young man named John. He goes to a very spirit filled church here in Florida. I have told him my story about how I died and asked him how it has affected his faith and relationship and need for God in his life.

He finds my story encouraging instead of discouraging. It helps bring him faith and belief. It brings hope to him. He considers himself a small flame.

This is a conversation we had one day . . .

John says, "My anointing is affected by my workplace and where I work. If I could give up my work place Gods anointing would be much stronger."

"Why do you feel the Satanists are trying to kill you?" I asked.

The boy next to my house is a Wicka Witch and in my dream I see him riding a small bike and he starts talking to me in my dream. I start shouting at him that Jesus is Lord and then all the snakes that are all over him are falling off and crawling away."

John, in another dream, "I remember being in a car. I see his dog and the dog starts to bark at me, letting me know that the boy is going to turn on me. Then I see a boa snake and it is wrapped around him in such a way that it seemed to be killing the boy."

John has a desire to go into street ministry and desires to help those that need it the most.

How has the story I told you added to your personal faith in God?

John accepted what happened to me. He sees how God is reaching out to me. He sees what God has done for me and how God is merciful and forgiving. John can see how I am being pulled back into Gods life. I find it interesting that he sees what is done to me and not himself.

John has decided to tell me a little bit about himself.

As a child in middle school and high school he was extremely picked upon and tormented by other children in an extreme way. He was taken to the point of thoughts of killing other children at school and murder and suicide during his young years.

What does this say about our society and environment?

"How did you keep from doing these things? What prevented it from happening? What did you learn that kept you from acting upon this pressure at school?" I asked him.

I give credit to the love of family and people that cared for me. If I had a bad family structure and the foundation that was taught to me by family was not there, the worst might have happened. No one outside my family really cared for me. I would have been lead to my destruction to the worst extent.

I prayed for a long time asking why I went through this suffering. I remember why. I had made fun of a Christian boy in elementary school, around the fifth grade. I believe that somehow what happened to me is related to my bullying a Christian boy in elementary school.

John's Faith

John believes that Jesus Christ is the Son of God. He believed this before he met me. John goes on to say that anyone who does not believe this is cursed. A Christian is blessed and not to be cursed. We allow curses of other to affect us. Faith is what is needed. People that throw curses are bad shots and instead of curing the one they intend they hurt others in the process.

The example of Jesus needs to be followed or others you will be led astray. As men of God we must influence others to teachings of Jesus and not be influenced by things of the world.

From the Gospel of Luke 4:11 ....
**He will give his angels charge concerning you to guard you,
And,
On their hands they will bear you up, lest you strike your foot against a
stone, . . .**

JAHAN'S FALL...

Working at the restaurant has introduced me to some very interesting people. I literally met Jahan through God. Jahan had just started working and we did a night shift together. God was prompting me to go and tell Jahan what had happened to me and also to go and listen to what had happened to him. God gave me no glimpse of what was going to be told to me just to go and speak about my story and listen to what had happened to him.

I started the conversation with these few words. You have a faith about you, there is something inside you that is a faith in God and God wishes me to tell you what had happened to me. Jahans story and supernatural event is extremely interesting. Jahan fell from a height of about 3 stories into a pile of rubble and solid debris while he was working on a building one day. He tells me that he fell into this pile of debris and landed flat on his back as if he were laying flat on a bed. He stood up with out a scratch. He stood up without a broken bone and without a scratch. He stood up expecting to be severely hurt. I hope to get him to sit down with me and talk about it more because there is always more to the story. There is not just the physicality of what happened but there is also the emotional and the spiritual aspect of action. How did Jahan feel and what did this say to his spirit.

I recently found a point of interest in the scriptures that apply to Jahans life. I found this scripture in Luke 4: 9-11. **"He will give His Angels charge concerning you to guard you and on their hands they will bear you up, lest you strike your foot against a stone."**

Now in this passage of the bible in Luke 4, you find the devil tempting Jesus. The Devil is actually using the authentic scriptures against Jesus and trying to use Gods scriptures to tempt Jesus. The Scripture that the Devil is quoting is an actual scripture although the devil is perverting it in this context. As we go on in this text of Luke we see Jesus tell the devil that you should not tempt the Lord your God.

Now here is the strange thing, the scripture that the devil quoted is a real quote. Jahan actually lived it out in his life. Jahan did not jump off the building and Jahan was not pushed off the building, it was simply an accident. This is the true intent of the scripture that the devil was quoting. God has given his angels charge over us to protect us against accidents and injury when we are put here to serve Gods purpose.

Young Angel of the streets . . .

There is a young girl at work that has been very curious about my book She has been watching me write it without knowing what it is about and curiosity is killing her. She is young, only 16 but has an amazing story to tell and I suspect a very eventful life ahead of her. At first I would not tell her what the book was about because of many reasons. Then I remembered a few certain passages of scripture about how Jesus was glad that God revealed himself to certain people of economic classification and not others. Let me extrapolate, "And the angels appeared to the Sheppard's of the field and they were sorely afraid . . ." Angels told the Sheppard's of the field about the birth of Jesus and not the Pharisees in the temple. The Sheppard's of the field were considered 3rd class citizens and were not "worthy" to enter into the temple and worship. SO . . . . God told them **first** about Jesus. This is a very, very noticeable characteristic of God and children of God and happens throughout the bible. So, I decided to not let this persons age make me prejudice about whom I reveal what has happened to me so I found myself telling her about my suicide one day and then she told me about her brush with death, which came to me as a complete shock. I have never met someone so young and healed or resurrected or prevented from death.

This young lady was stabbed in the stomach at the age of 12. She has told me some very disturbing things about the type of life that she has been forced to endure and I thought that I would share it.

Here is the story of a young lady that has been forced to endure too much at such an early age; her name is Angel.

Somehow, someway a 12-year-old girl found herself in an ally and was stabbed in the stomach area. She said that she fell to the ground and blacked out. As she blacked out she remembers herself being pulled up and out of her body and saw her body as if she was standing next to it. She remembers a light, a bright white light and then remembers being woken up in the hospital.

This has all the characteristics of a classic NDE if those reading this book would take the time to research the events.

From the Gospel of Thomas:

(25) Jesus says:
(1) "Love your brother like your life!
(2) Protect him like the apple of your eye!"

(25) Jesus said, "Love your brother like your soul, guard him like the pupil of your eye."
25. Jesus said, "Love your friends like your own soul, protect them like the pupil of your eye."

There are three different translations to the gospel of Thomas and I thought that I would include all three here for you to view . . . these translations have a direct bearing on the passages below that follow this.

7/4/2006

Where am I today? I have recently started taking in the homeless and people off the streets. I have 2 new roommates that occupy the couch and the reclining chair. I will not give those people names but will try and tell you what I have learned about God and myself in the process of doing these things for other people.

I know that the average church going person would never consider taking in someone off the street corner and letting them sleep on the couch or in their house. People are more in love with their stuff and concerned with their things than they are with the hearts and lives of others. These two persons have some very different beliefs and views on life, to say the least. I did not judge them. I did not take them into my home based on what their faith is, I took them in based on my faith. These people could believe in pink elephants or Satan himself. I am not called to act or judge others by what they believe, we are called to act on what we believe. I act on my faith and do according to my faith. It is my intention to allow nothing to disturb my faith. I intend to only act on my faith and be put in situations to allow God to let my faith grow towards God.

Jesus went to the outcasts of his society in his time and was chastised for it by the priests and people of his time. Good people expect to be accepted by God. Bad people hope to be accepted by God but neither two types of people can find a common ground to accept each other.

I often felt that God wanted me to start a ministry to the homeless but I never knew how God was going to provide for me so that I could provide for them. Perhaps the ministry that I start will resemble the book of acts where all the people pitched in and took care of each other.

You might be wondering how I met these two people, I will tell you. I was doing my job one day as a carpenter and asked to take one of my friends home and tried to give him a ride but he said to me that he had no where to go because he was living on the streets. In that moment I decided that I really could not allow this to happen and told him to come home with me. The other person living here is in a different situation where he was forced to leave his home because of behavior from roommates such as drugs, alcohol and prostitution and fighting. The basic moral of where he lived was in a downward spiral so I invited him to come and leave that situation behind.

They are both here and we go through the daily routine of life together. Where it will lead I have no idea. If God does have a ministry for the homeless planned for me it has not been revealed to me yet. I would give it a name, "**The least of these my brethren**" naming it after the passage that Jesus said," when you do this to the least of these my brethren you do this also for me". This is from the book of Matthew 25.

I have also seen a definite pattern or line being drawn between two different types or classes of people. People go to church, get clean and then turn their back on other people and simply start to think and reason that God does not want them to get involved with people that are judged to be filthy by our society. Does anyone else see this but me? Let me put it another way. People keep telling me to stay away from these type of people because they cannot be reached. I'm not looking for them, meaning the homeless derelicts that dive into a bottle every day to numb their hearts and minds to the earth, I'm looking for God and I am trying to find God by doing and by acting. So if you really are trying to learn what I have learned and want to know what I know then go get a homeless person and take them into your home, in Gods name, and see what they teach you instead of seeing what they might steal from your living room. See what they can teach you instead of what you will need to provide for them to get "back on their feet". See what you can learn by letting them live with you or is it impossible to see past your own superficial prejudice of others in our society? I dare you to get involved with God in such a way that you are put in what you judge to be harms way. See what you find. I promise you that it will be more than interesting to say the least. I am now on the look out for expanding my home in a way that allows me to take in one more person.

I recently found a friend of mine digging in a dumpster for food and I could not stand the sight of this also. I asked the people that were in the car with me to stop the car and I got out of the car and asked him if he wanted to get some food and told him that he did not need to dig in dumpsters for food. He decided to get on his bike and ride away instead of letting me give him some food. I still do not understand this. Perhaps this is the next person to come to my house to live. I would enjoy this. It would make coming back to earth worth it.

What have I learned from these interactions with other people . . .

I have not been deluding myself thinking that I am going to save the world. I do not have a messiah complex as some might think. I know that some people cannot be reached and no matter what you do others will still not learn. People will learn in their time, not when I come or do not come into the lives of others. People have their own rate of growth in all aspects, emotional and spiritual.

I help others for a reason that others never consider. I am chasing after Jesus and following after Jesus and trying to find what he found and trying to know and learn what he learned. Jesus went to the people that are shunned in society, the prostitutes, the drug addicts and the alcoholics. I am searching for Jesus, not messianic fantasies about saving all the homeless or drug addicts or what have you. By doing as Jesus did I have an understanding now that I did not have before, not about the people that I help but about the Savior himself. God always goes to the 3rd class citizen first, the Sheppard's in the field, the drunks and tax collectors, the prostitutes and other people that are always shunned. It all comes back to the love. God is love without condition and always does this and gives this example time and time again. So, I am not pursuing the people that I help for their sakes although I am doing this also, I am pursuing these people to learn about God and how God loves people.

7/26/2006

One of my guests in my grandmother's house has left recently. We I found him he was taking a bath in the ocean and sleeping outside every night. He has left my house and is on his way to visit his mother. He has a bank account, which he acquired while at my house and has money in it that he saved. He has not slept outside since we met. I do not know what choices he will make while gone, I can only state the circumstances of how he left. He left on good terms and with prospects and potential that he was pursuing. He gave himself goals and I gave him goals while here and he did what I asked. One day I asked all the guys to get a bank account and start saving as a safety net if something happens and we all must leave. They did it. I see progress and I see people being elevated through hard work and perseverance and good choices being made and done.

Yesterday I spent the day talking with a pastor going over the idea of starting a non-profit organization to help the situation of homeless in this area. I will name it after the passage of Matthew 25: 31-46 "The least of these my brethren". I hope to have all my paperwork filed by Christmas. I am starting to document each situation closely as the people begin to pass through these doors. Each person has a different story to tell. I will do what I can for everyone that I meet. All I can do is simply share what I have, spiritual and physical. If I wanted a roommate to simply charge rent, I would put an advertisement in the paper. There are real people with real needs in this society and small community here. I intend to do what I can for those that I encounter.

Perhaps a few years from now you will be able to find my shelter on the Internet filled with photos of all the people that have passed through my doors and you will see their story of how they were down and helped themselves back up. I am not going to build this shelter, they will. Last night I interviewed someone that is being evicted from their drug dealer filled prostitute ridden neighborhood and he is sitting on my porch telling me about how he was looking for a tent at the local Wal mart. His problems were stopped before they started, he is moving in this week.

A lot of upper class people have no idea what it is like to live in these types of areas so I will be sure to write some of the stories that he tells me about where he came from. He was telling me last night about his previous situation and how people that are his neighbors would steal things from him while he watched, such as bicycles and other things. He has had people try and force their way into his home randomly at any given time of day. He has had to call the police on many occasions. The drug dealers and prostitutes are staying though, and he is getting evicted. I find that a truism of this world and a wonderful haiku as an explanation of this world not Gods heaven.

From the Gospel of Thomas . . .

You have all three translations here

Jesus says:

**(1) "Come to know what is in front of you, and that which is hidden from you will become clear to you.
(2) For there is nothing hidden that will not become manifest."**

**Jesus said, "Know what is in front of your face, and what is hidden from you will be disclosed to you. For there is nothing hidden that will not be revealed. [And there is nothing buried that will not be raised.]"
Jesus said, "Recognize what is in your sight, and that which is hidden from you will become plain to you. For there is nothing hidden which will not become manifest."**

131

7/30/2006

A friend of mine was having some trouble and I wrote her a letter so I thought that I would insert it here and perhaps other people could relate to what is going on here. See if this helps you either now or in the future at some point. This exert from the Gospel of Thomas applies to what I have written in this letter and in the first paragraph.

Stephaine,

When you can see what you are doing to yourself you will be able to see how to stop and why you should stop doing these things to yourself.

You have desires and needs and appetite and all these things. We all do. You deserve to be filled and fulfilled in your heart and body but there are certain things that you must take into consideration.

You think that you have made a choice but you have not made a real choice yet.

When you can see the outcome and all the potentials and all the possibilities and know the avenues of destruction and the avenues of creation then you will be able to make the choice to stop doing certain things in your life. The only choice you have made is to take a path of self-destruction. The only choice you have made so far is to continue to hurt your self and spirit.

I have discovered so many things, I wish you were with me to discover them because these things that I have discovered are things that empower people and not take away their power over themselves. While helping people and watching over them I can see their choices being made and see how they make blind choices that are based on emotion and the wrong thing and wrong philosophy.

You are seeing yourself now. You are seeing what you really are deep below the surface and also on the surface. Soon you will become disgusted with what you see and when you get so feed up with yourself and what you have allowed yourself to become then you will want to change and see why you need to change yourself.

You are seeing yourself without the influence of your husband and a mate. You are seeing yourself and you are the only one that you can blame right now so you will see what you are and what you have become and have been becoming for years now and did not know it. Everything grows, darkness grows and light grows. They both grow inside us at the same time.

It is written to let the wheat grow with the weeds and God will sort them out. You don't need to wait that long. You can take action and control in your life now if you want to, that is the real purpose of free will. What you are doing with your free will is simply abusing it and making wrong choices to go down paths of self-destruction based your emotional state of being right now.

Choosing to do what you are doing now, sexually, is an exercise in free will but it is also an exercise in self-starvation and self-destruction and self-mutilation but you are not doing this to the physical, you are doing this to the spiritual.

You are about to make the transition from blind faith and a faith that is without knowledge to having an educated faith in God and you will be saying at last I understand why you want me to not do these things and then you will have an educated faith and know why and your heart will be able to walk away from certain things toward what you really want and need and that is to be fulfilled and loved and give love and be close to someone and just get complete satisfaction from someone that just holds you while you sleep.

I have several scriptures that I want to share with you and I also have some things that I wrote that I want to share with you about love and our spirit. These are so powerful things.

Here is the bottom line. You do not value yourself. You devalue yourself. You hold God in great esteem and in high regard and God is sacred but you hold yourself in sacrilege. You consider yourself to be something that is not sacred. So there is the conflict within you. You value God but do not value yourself. God values you but you do not value yourself. So there is the fault and the inability to connect. So what should you do? Become a being that gives itself a value. Hold yourself to be sacred and don't pollute yourself. So what must you do? Begin to value yourself as a sacred being that refuses to defile itself.

When you begin to hold yourself as something of value and decide that you would not want to defile yourself or pollute yourself then you will be able to walk away from just about anything.

You are not expected or demanded to be perfect but you are expected to stop doing the things that you know are wrong and you must have complete knowledge as to why you should not do certain things. You know what you are doing. You know how it makes you feel. It feels good at first but later the feelings of guilt and being filthy and all those things associated with that feeling come to heart and mind.

So you will be given the knowledge that will let you stop participating in certain things in your life and you will be strong enough to walk away from what you are doing now if you choose this path for your life.

7/31/2006

I have decided to start a new book, a closer detailing of the things that occur with the homeless people that I encounter. Here are a few exerts from this book that I will work and write and live out in the days to come.

Chapter one:
Detailed experiences of first meetings with the homeless taken in . . .

I have decided to write about the human aspect, the everyday incidentals that occur and the personal aspect of what I am doing by bringing in the homeless into my house and taking them in off the streets. I have decided to call these people subjects and give them all numbers since what I am doing requires a certain amount of sanitizing for their protection. These are real people that I interact with and live with on a daily basis and I have no intention of turning this into a gossip column but I am trying to relay the human aspect and human characteristics of the choices that these people make and the choices that I make.

Subject One . . . The first person I asked to
take off the streets with God in mind . . .

It was a sunny day and very nice. I was working out of a labor hall and had not started taking in the homeless yet. The thought of it had not occurred to me yet to do such a thing. I was taking in people but not in an organized fashion.

I was giving a ride home to a friend of mine and I asked him where can I let you out and he said anywhere in town. I said why is that and he said that he was living outside on the streets and has nowhere to go. I stood there for a moment and something inside me became furious. Something inside me said enough was enough. I then looked back up at him and said when I am around there is no reason or need for you to sleep outside. I invited him home with me and it has led me to where I am now.

Subject 2 . . .
The shower in the front yard and the wet shorts and no church

I was stopping at the gas station getting gas and then I looked up and saw a man digging through the dumpster at the gas station getting food that was still wrapped up and just thrown away by the manager of the store.

Well, I did not like what I saw so I thought that I would simply get involved. I walked over to him slowly and just asked him if he would like to come over for a cookout later that night and he did. We had barbeque chicken and spaghetti. He did not stay that night and seems to insist on staying outside so I thought I would not try and argue him out of his choices he made for himself.

The next time we would meet was a few days later, in my front yard. I came home to find him sleeping out side my front door. He sat there writing and having food and just spent the day under my front awning. He was writing notes constantly but I have no idea what he could be writing about all day long. Then he decide to take a nap and just pulled out his bed role and feel asleep on the ground. The other guys that came home stepped around him and over him to get inside. He agreed to go to church with us that night but never made it. He decided to instead take a bath with my garden hose and got his clothes all wet and could not go to church.

So where was I during all this? I offered him a spot on the couch but he declined. I offered him a shower inside but he also declined. I asked him if he wanted many things and declined. I even offered a new pair of shorts so he could attend church but he said no to hat as well.

I hope I see him again. I spent the day talking with this person and I found him wise and insightful. I guess this is why people are called the salt of the earth. I never new what that term meant until one day I found a scripture explaining it. Ancient people gave wisdom a nickname and they called it salt, they referred to "wisdom" as "salt". It is an interesting concept that wisdom when added gives a situation flavor and substance.

A friend in the dumpster, running away
Subject 3 . . .

I was riding down the street with a lady friend and I saw something very peculiar that I had to ask her to stop the car and let me out. A person that I know was climbing into a dumpster and actually digging for food. I know this person. This person has been in my personal vehicle many times and we have spent many a day at work together and we have had lunch together on several occasions. I had to stop, there was nothing else for me to do other than turn my back on a friend and I don't do that.

We stopped the car and I got out and went over to him and took him by the hand. It seemed that he recognized me but what happened later still perplexes me.

I asked him to simply come with me and that I would buy him some food and fix it for him and he agreed. As I turned and went back to the car to say good bye to my friends which were on their way to the beach the friend in the dumpster decided to jump on his bicycle and start pedaling the other way and ran away.

I really don't know what happened, one minute I was on my way to the beach with the baby and some friends then we see another friend of mine digging in a dumpster and then before I can get him some real food, he rides off as fast as he can. I did what I could but still feel bad. I feel bad because I know that he is still out there somewhere, looking for food and just wandering, I see him from time to time around town. We will meet again. Perhaps next time will be better.

The drug addict in the driveway, smoking crack
Subject 4 . . .

I have never met a young lady like this before in my life. She was very beautiful but at the same time looked like a skeleton from drug use.

She has been to my house twice and both times were very heart breaking. The heart always breaks and cracks a little when you meet someone that needs so much and accepts so little.

Subject 5&6 . . .
Late night visiting, drunk and hungry . . .

It was late and someone came knocking. It was a traveling guest that come by so often. He brought another homeless person that was sleeping in their van for whatever reason. They stopped in and wanted something to eat. I fixed them a sandwich and two burritos that I had in the freezer and bought the day before. They were too late for dinner or I would have had some chicken for them. They stayed and talked for a few minutes, 20 minutes at the most. I told one of the men that I want the word to start circulating on the street that if he finds someone that is truly in need of a place and wants to get in off the streets then bring them to me. I will make room. Both these people were street people, each with a different story. It was nice to be able to give someone some food in this manner. It felt as if God were visiting me as well as these men. The one homeless person told me that he was going to bring me a $5 bill so it can be my first donation to be framed. I look forward to that moment and I will frame it along with the drawings that I made of God when I first set eyes on God. When I first set eyes on God I did not go blind, in fact I did not want to turn my gaze away and look anywhere else.

For those of you that do not know what it means to sleep outside here are some of the places that people sleep while wandering around in our society.

These are authentic places that were described to me by people from the streets.

> Buildings closed, closed down or abandoned . . .
> Anywhere out of sight . . .
> Under the awning outside at a funeral home . . .
> Under a bridge or overpass . . .
> Woods, tent . . .
> Outside a church in the doorway and could not get in . . .
> Bus benches, . . .
> Roof top of buildings . . .

CHAPTER 11

STEWARDSHIP OF THE EARTH . . .

What has this world come? Who can we blame? We have only ourselves to blame. We dump atomic waste into the ocean. We plant atomic waste underground. Power plants are not buildings that produce electricity, they are buildings that produce nuclear waste and the by-product is electricity. Why do people try to justify an Evil act with a perceived and illusion of Good that is the outcome?

The atmosphere is being depleted in a way that we must soon create machines to put back what is being destroyed. The ozone layer is being burned away. We have machines that destroy the ozone and then we build machines the create ozone and let them fight it out in the atmosphere.

Abortion clinics are killing and killing and killing with no end in sight. If each baby killed were a brick what would be the size of the wall being built?

Every possible thing that we are to be held responsible for is being taken away with a convenient quick solution. People do things but are never held responsible. Divorce rate is almost going backwards. What does this mean; people make promises but never intend to keep them but don't mind getting other people to commit to things they never intend to commit to keeping. The person with a lack of commitment is usually the one that is asking for the marriage and then that same person is asking for the divorce.

We are systematically taught to love our cars and TV sets and VCR and DVD players and all things that cannot love you back. This is idol worship for those of you that don't know it. Money is the new false idol and we love it with all our hearts and all the things that money can bring especially the perceived power over other people.

What are we stewards of in this world? We are good stewards of perpetuating destructive behavior on every level.

Slavery is still an issue. If we are not slaves to each other then we are all slaves to money.

Which means the 1% of the population that owns the money is enslaving us all through systematic structuring of our society. Systematic financial structuring keeps the poor people poor and the rich with a constant flow of income. If a war arose where the poor formed and army and the rich had to defend themselves what would that be like? 98% of the planet is dirt poor.

Christians throughout the world are still being killed for their faith.

So what does it mean in essence to be killed for faith in God? You are being killed because you believe in love, and honesty among other things. God is Love.

The question is who is going to start making the effective change to get love back into the world? How can God ever expect to come back here except in a blaze of fury as described in the book of revelations? Does a loving God have a loving home that is in order to come home to or does a loving God have a house in disorder and destruction to come home and visit? God does not accept excuses. God does have forgiveness but people must repent first. Forgiveness can't take place without repentance. We have left God no choice but fury. We force Gods hand and do not know it. If we receive anything else other than Gods fury and hell then it is a credit to Gods mercy and grace and love and not our own intrinsic value.

CHAPTER 12

JUDGMENT DAY

I have often heard many pastors in many different churches say that God forgives and forgets. There is no such thing as forgive and forget with God. Jesus himself spoke of Judgment Day. He spoke of judgment day when he sent the disciples off into the towns to heal and minister. The very nature of the word judgment means that there is an accountability of actions that has been taken. The statement forgive and forget is a contradiction to the word judgment day.

People that have died and have been resurrected or sent back to life on earth go through judgment day also. These people refer to it as something different, they refer to it as a life review. Now before I explain about the life review or judgment day you will wonder if I had a life review when I was dead and I will have to say no. I had my judgment day while still alive before being dead and before committing suicide. Now, the next few statements that I make will be a jumble of emotions and we must always remember that when dealing with emotions they do not make sense or are rational they are simply what we feel at the time and make perfect sense at the time we are having them. So while I was being put through the pain of loosing my family it became a living hell and was the most horrible feelings that I have ever felt to date. When the first thought of committing suicide came into mind the pain was gone and it actually felt better. I made a commitment to myself to end this pain inside me and I felt relief. Then I began to interact with God and God started to show me myself and show me exactly what I was and what people are from Gods eyes and then I really wanted to put and end to everything and the pain became much worse than it ever was from the start. Being shown the truth of what we are is not a very pleasant sight to see. It is like viewing a form of hell or a form of damnation or subtle separation from God.

Some very interesting points of interest about the nature of God while showing a person how God views us is that God is interested in me learning about me and what I do and how my actions or words fall upon the hearts of others. God holds us responsible to what we do. God does not tell us about what other people do to us. God tells you about you and what you need to change to get yourself fixed. So if you are in a relationship with a person that seldom or never takes responsibility for their actions and always tells you that you are wrong then the relationship is one-sided. Each person must be held accountable for what they do or did, not what they think someone else did or what someone else is doing. God does not need you to tell God what Johnny did last Tuesday when no one was looking.

By Jesus himself we are directed NOT to judge others. We are in fact directed to keep our own sight clean and leave the other people alone.

If you are really interested in learning about the Near Death Experience and the term life review then I suggest going to the internet and research many NDE testimonies and listen to what the whole body of people have not say not just my limited view from my life. There are several NDE survivors that explain judgment day or the life review much better than I ever could. If I could sum it all up in some very candid phrases it would go like this:

God is going to take you aside moments after you die and show you your entire life from beginning to end and then allow you to touch and feel all the good things and bad things and you will see yourself from the eyes or emotional view point of every person that you ever met in your life and you will get to feel all the pain that you have ever given to someone and this will not be metaphorical it will in fact be literal. God is going to make you the judge of your own life and give you the ability to see yourself through omnipresence of others and also through omni-emotions of all those around you. You will literally become all those people that you have hurt in your life and experience word for word pain for pain and moment for moment whatever you have given. Then at that moment you will know the true need for Jesus and the sacrifice that was made for us on the cross. Then you will know what Gods plan was for Jesus when God led Jesus to die for us so that we may also return to the father in heaven.

If you wish to know more about this then you must do a lot more research than anything that I could write here. Do the research, get involved and search for answers that make sense to you. Get the videos of life after death experiences and watch them and really listen. Get onto the Internet and search the topics and read the testimonies of hundreds of people that are from all walks of life and all say the same thing. We all have a very difficult time explaining these events. Search. Search is another word for pray if you really look into the definition of the word pray and what it means.

Everybody is a friend of Jesus when . . .

Have you ever noticed how everyone is a friend of Jesus when Jesus is out healing the sick and the blind and the crippled and the lepers and doing things for everyone? Has anyone also noticed that when it comes time to be chastised by the lord and Jesus starts telling you what is wrong with you and wants to chastise you people abandon Jesus? This happened frequently through out the gospels, disciples were always leaving when they disagreed with his teaching and he was always openly ridiculed and chastised for telling people the simple truth about God and Gods realm.

This is a stark contrast to the same person isn't it, or is it? One minute Jesus is healing people and the next he is tearing them down. What is that about? The chastisement of God is a Good thing.

Secrets are hidden in the relationship of John the Baptist and Jesus and the judgment day and God convicting people of their sin.

The beginning of the path back to God and Jesus is repentance. What do we repent from? What do we turn toward? These are the things that God will show you if God decides to have a living relationship and interaction with you in your life. We look back at the bible and just see a wonderful story of characters and we have all the lines memorized and know every word by heart and know what it written that this person did and that person did but the simple fact is that we really don't. We don't know the human aspect of it and to put this in a perspective I will tell you about the things I have written in this book and how it affects me personally.

I recently picked up a homeless person that was living under a bridge and brought her into my home. God directed me to do this. God asked me to do this. I also agreed to do this. Now as you read this you might say "oh how wonderful . . ." "What a nice relationship he must have with God." Now this is just not reality. The reality of it is that it is past noon and this person is in there snoring on the couch. What is that all about? This person promised to do things such as work around the house in exchange for staying here. I take care of her and she takes care of me. This has not happened yet. I have been doing most of the taking care of someone and she is still snoring. There is talking about doing something, there is the ideal about doing something; there is the reality and human aspect of doing something. The reality is that she snores and is awake all night and goes to the bathroom 15 times a night and it is very, very irritating and it has only been 2 days. So this is the reality of it and you need to look at yourself and the fantasy world that you live in within your mind and rethink your concepts of God.

God convicting a person of their sin is no joke and is very painful. God asking someone to repent is the exact opposite of what you want to do. John the Baptist openly chastised King Herod and lost his head because he shouted for Gods will to be done, not the will and desires of the flesh of men. Jesus did not think or imagine dying on the cross, he did not pretend or say wow what a wonderful idea, he got serious beyond our understanding of everything and went and did what God asked. So the question is are you ready to do the hard thing for God and for others. Are you ready to suffer to learn what is right? Are you ready to suffer for God? Now on the other end of my new houseguest, do I enjoy her company? Yes. Is she fun to be around and a pleasant person? Yes. So it is a very human situation, accepting the good and the bad in each situation on a daily basis. Then God comes along and things get much more interesting because God is interested in the spirit of a person not the flesh of a person. So what does it mean to be healed by Jesus one minute and chastised by Jesus the next minute? They are both needed and both very important. In my opinion the chastisement of the lord is much more important. Without Gods correction and constant attention to keep us going in the right direction then we stray and get lost from the path. Judgment waits for us all and must be accepted like everything else and must happen or you simply can't grow beyond what you are at this moment. God show you yourself and teaches you about you. I know a lot of people that talk and talk and talk about God but when God calls them to repent from certain things it's a real problem for them and for others. An easy example of this is to try and live with an alcoholic that refuses that they have a problem. Try living with a crack addict prostitute that has sex for drugs and cares about nothing other than her drugs. Those people are someone's daughter and son and someone's brother and sister. Someone somewhere loves them and misses them. They refuse to repent and turn away from self-destructive behavior. God loves these people. There are other problems that are much more subtle and much more destructive and people also refuse to repent and turn away from these behaviors as well.

Once again you are presented with a mystery and it will be a mystery that changes right in front of your eyes just like it has changed in front of mine. I once thought I had it all figured out. I thought death was absolute and you do it one time and that is it, well even this concept of our reality was broken in me because I did die and I am still here, still very much resentful of this fact because I still do not want to be here because I know what this place is, I really cant tell you though, I am incapable of describing it.

Now let me share one more point of interest with the concept of judgment day and the NDE event called the life review. First let me go back to scripture.

From the Gospel of Luke 6: 12-26

> Blessed are you who are poor, for yours is the kingdom of God
>
> Blessed are you who hunger now for you shall be satisfied
>
> Blessed are you who weep now for you will laugh
>
> Blessed are you when men hate you and insult you and reject your name as evil because of the son of man, rejoice in that day and leap for joy because great is the reward in heaven for that is how their fathers treated the prophets
>
> Woe to you who are rich for you have already received your comfort
>
> Woe to you who are well fed for you will go hungry
>
> Woe to you who laugh now for you will mourn and weep
>
> Woe to you when All men speak well of you for that is how they treated the false prophets

People often think that they know what this passage means but they are mistaken, some people might understand this and others do not and some comprehend but not completely. I think that covers the spectrum of understanding so let me say what has been brought to mind about these passages, which have been named the "Be" attitudes.

These passages are a prediction of what is to come when a person dies and goes to heaven. These passages are not telling us about now but about what is to come when we go into our personal judgment day. If you take the time to look at what has been pointed out in each persons life review and IF you take the time to notice what has been shown to each person in their life review as being truly valued in heaven you will notice that each person will line up directly with these statement made by Jesus. These blessings are also in line with the concept of the man that was sent back and the passage about the one that was great here on earth but very small in heaven.

So take the time to see and watch the videos and really listen to what the people say that was important in their life reviews and also listen to what they thought was important before they died and you will see some startling contrasts. The essence or common thing that is learned is that what we thought was important in this world is in reality not important, and what we dismiss as unimportant in this world is completely important in reality. God is love and a living being of pure love therefore his judgments and conclusions will be based on a gauge or standard of love or absence of love in each and every action that a person takes. I wish that I could really explain what I am trying to tell you but once again I find it difficult to put into words so please watch the videos and look at these passages and see what the spirit shows you. I will try to give a few points of interest to upset your curiosity enough to make you search for some real knowledge. I will refer to the NDE sites and paraphrase what people tell about their life review and what they learned about real value in heaven and our eternal life that is to come after this one.

After reviewing the NDE testimonies of what happens at a life review there is a common denominator of circumstances and it is this. That which we deem unimportant in this world is very, very important to us after we leave this world and go into the light or the next life. That which we deem as important here is seldom considered significant or of any value there.

It all comes down to being selfless or choosing to be selfish. Selfless people of love give without thought of reward or condition of what they are giving. Selfish people discourage themselves from even considering the possibility of giving to other people even when people are in desperate need right in front of their eyes. Do I give the homeless man a sandwich or do I not give the homeless man a sandwich? If you do not know why you need to feed another human a simple scrap of food then you can consider yourself lost and in the outer darkness of yourself.

CHAPTER 13

THE YIN AND YANG OF CONVERSATION

I cannot rewrite the bible with these short experiences and this is not even an attempt to try. What I am trying to do is simply share the mysteries that I have discovered while on this journey.

The concept of yin and yang is thousands of years old. I have only recently started applying this concept of yin and yang to the art of speaking and listening to conversation as in reference to people that talk to me and also the written word of the bible.

Lets start with a small example of yin and yang applied to conversation:

There is an old question that is designed to tell the personality of someone. Is the glass half empty or half full? What ever a person responds will give insight into their personality and if they are an optimist or a pessimist. Lets take this question one step further.

The glass is neither half empty nor is it half full. The glass is simultaneously half empty and also half full. This is a complete answer that leaves no room for lack of knowledge and no room for doubt.

People often speak in half-truths and operate on a limited amount of knowledge to make difficult choices. Saying the glass is half full is a half-truth. This concept of yin and yang applied to language is very informative with what is being spoken and written while a person is on a quest or search for knowledge.

Yin and yang are opposites that balance each other and you cannot have one without the other. A complete answer to the question of half empty/half full is that they are both. Using this method we can see more completely what is being said to us through out the bible and also what is being said to us by other people.

The essence of the gospel of Jesus is this," Your captivity in sin is over, we are forgiven of sin and redeemed." So looking at this statement from a reverse angle it makes many statements. We are trapped in sin and some of us don't even know it. We are in a type of bondage that we are not aware of or even know about. We are probably closer to hell than heaven since there are no captives in heaven and there is no hidden knowledge in heaven.

So, lets apply this to a few phrases that are in the bible and see what presents itself. You can do this on your own while someone is speaking to you and you can do this while you are reading.

Lets start with some insight into the 10 commandments. What is the essence or simplest form of the 10 commandments? They are statements of action. The 10 commandments are statements of non-action or things not to do or things not to participate in. So having faith in the commandments is irrelevant if you are not willing to act and do these things, which means NOT DOING THESE THINGS LISTED IN THE COMMANDMENTS. Sometimes doing Gods "will" can mean not participating and not doing certain things. By telling us what not to do God is also telling is what to do simultaneously. This also gives insight into the noninterference of God.

I have noticed a pattern in the actions of God and Gods angels. They never seem to tell you exactly what to do, they show you things and let you decide for yourself or in the case of the commandments they tell you what not to do.

This type of yin/yang action can also be seen in the life of Jesus Christ. He was a person of action every day, every time not just a person of philosophy or tradition or belief/faith. He acted.

This brings me to a statement that is often read in the bible, "Faith without works is dead." The opposite of this is also true," Works without faith is dead." While reading the bible as I apply the yin/yang theory to things that were spoken by Jesus it gives me great insight into what is really being said which gives direction or a course of action to be taken by us. One of the greatest problems that Christians face is "what do we do?" We have faith but we do not know exactly what to do to release or express or give faith to God. We wander aimlessly throughout our lives believing but wondering what to do and it sometimes seems that when we ask God what to do all we get is silence and more silence.

So, how can I explain this concept further? I can't. All I can say is try it and see what you find. Study the concept of yin and yang as taught by those that wrote it and apply this concept of opposite balance to what is spoken to you and to what you say and to what you read in any given situation and see what strange facts are revealed to you as you look. This is a very enlightening tool and can be helpful when searching for truth and knowledge.

Let me put this as a directive or something to do. Seek both halves to make the whole or entirety of what someone is saying to you when they speak. Hear what they are saying without words as well as with words. See both halves of what is in front of you and both halves of what is being spoken to you so that you can have a clearer understanding of what is being said to you or the situation that you are caught within.

To give you another example . . .

To give you another example of the concept of the yin and yang of conversation I have written a passage in a different chapter and it is about something written within Corinthians. Now I do not want you to look at what I wrote, I want you to look at the opposites that are combined to make a complete knowledge of what is being said to you.

Look at the description of love and look at the description of the negative counterpart to love and you will have a complete knowledge of what love is and what love is not. This is why they say that God is above Good and Evil. If you only know and understand one of the counterparts then you have an incomplete knowledge. Here it is for you to look at in a different way.

Here is a passage from 1st Corinthians:
Corinthians 13: 4

Love is patient. Love is kind and is not jealous; love does not brag and is not arrogant, does not act unbecomingly, does not seek its own, is not provoked, does not take into account a wrong suffered, does not rejoice in unrighteousness, but rejoices with the truth; Love bears all things, believes all things, hopes all things and endures all things.

This is the word of the bible and the word of God. This word of God is a good beginning to describing the love of God although the concept of agape is not touched upon in this passage.

Let me tell you about this world and the love created by this world without Gods guidance and Gods help.

Love in this world is stalking. Love in this world is prejudice and is given upon conditions and criteria. Love in this world is a predator. Love in this world is given then quickly taken back. Love in this world wakes you up at 3 am to argue with your spouse. Love in this world keeps lists and holds grudges. Love in this world starts arguments. Love in this world cannot let go of anger. Love in this world creates paranoia and is paranoid. Love in this world creates a state of confusion and clouds the truth and a person's ability to reason. Love in this world is willing to tear down and kill for all the wrong reasons. Love in this world is a prison keeper and holds others prisoner in their own home and mind. Love in this world is vengeful and spiteful and jealous. No one is ever good enough for love in this world and no one is ever good enough for the one that claims to love them in this world. Love in this world helps perpetuate your problems with no end to the problems in sight. Love in this world is abusive and strikes you. Love in this world can be murder because men have murdered those they claim to love. Love in this world makes you a hypocrite. Love in this world causes you to deceive someone into loving you then abandon him or her when they need you the most. Love in this world is a lie. Love in this world causes mothers to put their babies into dumpsters after they are born. The list goes on and on but you do not need me to write it down because I know that somehow and in some way you have somehow lived out these things written here and could probably add to this list if you decided to add to it.

ONE FINAL EXAMPLE OF THE CONCEPT OF YIN AND YANG TO CONVERSATION

Here are some simple phrases that we all speak about God and never really understand or know what we are saying, we think we are speaking well wishes and happiness to others but here is one aspect of what we are really saying, first let me give you the phrases . . .

"May the Lord bless you and keep you . . ."

"May God have mercy on you . . ."

Now let's examine and apply the philosophy of yin/yang to the spoken word.

"May the Lord bless you and keep you", has very serious implications about the state of the Lord and also our state of being. If someone needs to bless you or bestow something on you it means that you are lacking and in desperation for something. May the Lord keep you means that either the Lord is in the habit of casting people out or down or we are in the habit of leaving and running away! Which one is it? See the negative and the positive of the statement being made to see the whole of what is being made and the dynamic of the situation. The exact opposite of this statement is that the Lord does not bless people and casts people down. This is why the statement asks the Lord to bless and keep you. The entire statement is built upon the contingency of the word "May" which is a question.

"May God have mercy on you", has some very serious implications about God and our state of being. The asking of God to have mercy means that we have done something that is wrong or destructive toward another individual or toward God, thus the need for mercy. The need for mercy means that someone has been wronged in someway. Asking God to have mercy means that you are in a situation that is in need and requires a being of higher power to help and intercede and provide. The exact opposite of the statement is that God is merciless and gives mercy infrequently, thus the need to ask for mercy. So what is really being said in these two statements? That is for you to decide what it is that you see. Do you want to see completely or partial aspects of everything being said to you.

These 2 statements also give insight into the environment that the person exists within. If a person needs to be kept or needs mercy or needs a blessing it gives insight into the fact we live in a violent environment with lack of provision in many ways.

So as you can see a large amount of information can be taken from the slightest fraction of information given.

Chapter 14

Falling short of the Glory of God

In a previous chapter I wrote about certain people that were affected by Gods influence using me. God used me to affect people's faith and add to their lives. So the question is how can I explain this and keep things clear and not cloud the issues?

God is the same each and every day. God is not going anywhere. God is not going to relocate heaven and not tell anyone. We are all different. If 100 people were told the same sentence those 100 people would all interpret that sentence differently.

For each and every person that receives God, there are thousands that do not receive the exact same living God of everything. The people that are ready to receive will. The people that do not want God will not be forced to receive God. The people that say they want God to help them and really do not want help will also not receive God.

The Gospel of Jesus is called the good news but let me tell you the not so good news about the exact same gospel. Jesus calls us to repent, and this is very, very bad news to some people in our society. It is extremely difficult for some to receive God because of their own actions. Alcoholics, drug addicts and other types of people like this have a very difficult time getting help and receiving anything from God because they need to stop pursuing their addictions and do as God asks them to do.

Jesus once said to a crowd of people let the one without sin cast the first stone. Then he asked the prostitute that was about to be stoned if her accusers were still there condemning her. The prostitute said no. Then Jesus said; then neither do I condemn you. Then Jesus said, go and sin no more.

This was an extremely bold move on the part of the Savior. First he told people in a very loud and very quiet way, stop condemning each other. He also said with his actions, stop stoning people and killing them in the name of sin/God. Then the most radical thing that he said in my opinion is that he told the woman to go and sin no more. He was reinforcing the concept of repentance. This is the trap that alcoholics and drug addicts and people with various types of conditions fall into. They beg for forgiveness but still refuse to repent and stop doing what they are doing. Jesus did not say to the prostitute go and charge double your price now. He did not say, go and turn as many tricks as you can and be a full time prostitute. He did not say, I forgive you and it's ok to just keep on getting it and keep on tricking or prostituting. He simply and plainly said go and sin no more. Stop it. Cut it out. Quit it. God has a no tolerance policy. However, God also has a policy that is extremely abused and that is that God allows us to sin and sin until we finally learn our lesson and get it right and do finally in the end after a great deal of hardship, we finally repent and say oh, Jesus I get it now, I should not do that and I should not have been doing that all this time and me not doing that was you telling me something for my own good.

So for each person that has a happy or interesting or supernatural story there are hundreds that do not. I have personally told and personally "rebuked" alcoholics and told them specifically to stop and go to A.A. meetings and get help and they very adamantly refuse to the point of violence. I have also done this with drug addicts and people that smoke and all kinds of patterns of self-destructive behavior. I have noticed that people fight for their perceived right to self-destruct and self destroy their life. I have a right to drink and smoke and drug up and I have this right to destroy myself. This is the common argument. God has a very different point of view. If it's self destructive or destructive to others then you must stop doing these things immediately.

Testimonies of profit . . .

I have also noticed other lines that are being drawn within the church and its people and there are two very distinctive patterns that are emerging and I wonder if anyone ever takes time to notice these things.

My real question is who is answering these prayers? Is God or the devil answering the prayers of these people in the church? I don't know. I only notice the patterns that emerge. Here is the pattern and what is happening. If you walk into any church you will always find someone with a story that goes like this: "I was once a drug addict, alcoholic, drug dealer, you fill in the blank, and then I gave my life to Jesus and I got a better job, an new house a new car and life is wonderful." That's a nice story but lets take a look at the bible and see what the book of acts has to say about this.

In the book of acts nowhere does it say that any of the apostles that followed Jesus got a better life and a better job and "prospered". The apostle Paul refers to himself as a slave or bondservant to God and Jesus. I also do not remember anywhere in the bible where Jesus says to follow him to financial prosperity. Jesus does however; preach about self-invoked self-sacrificing servitude to others and a life of selfless behavior. Jesus calls us to serve others and in serving others we serve our selves. So how is it that this God we all seek and serve and seek to know and seek to love in on one side of the fence giving away free Cadillac's and new lives and houses and better jobs and then on the other side calling people to be self-sacrificing and giving to the point of dying for others with no regard for themselves. Who is really following Jesus? Pay attention next time and listen to the story of people in the church and then look at the bible and see where God sent Jesus and the apostles. They were always sent into situations to serve others, help others, bring light and bring out the truth so it may be done and told and spoken out loud. Jesus didn't go to Jerusalem to get a new house and a new ass to ride up and down the streets on Sunday. He went there to die for others. You decide what is going on. You tell me if you see the same things that I see.

CHAPTER 15

INTERPRETATIONS TO GOSPEL SAYINGS . . .

These are for you and your faith to decide . . . .

I refuse to stand in for the definitions of Gospel sayings and chose your definition for you. What you believe and what you do and the action that you chose to take is for you to decide and to work out with God. I can only tell you what has happened to me and share with you the events that unfolded in my life. Something similar or not so similar may take place in your life depending on what is truly in your heart. All I can say is look hard look deep and look long and try to make good choices. Don't let this world of illusions choose for you. Don't let another person choose for you. Don't let your emotions choose for you. Make choices with a sober spirit and mind.

I do have a few things that came to mind lately after talking with some friends about relationships.

Here is a passage from 1st Corinthians:
Corinthians 13: 4

Love is patient. Love is kind and is not jealous; love does not brag and is not arrogant, does not act unbecomingly, does not seek its own, is not provoked, does not take into account a wrong suffered, does not rejoice in unrighteousness, but rejoices with the truth; Love bears all things, believes all things, hopes all things and endures all things.

This is the word of the bible and the word of God. This word of God is a good beginning to describing the love of God although the concept of agape is not touched upon in this passage.

Let me tell you about this world and the love created by this world without Gods guidance and Gods help.

Love in this world is stalking. Love in this world is prejudice and is given upon conditions and criteria. Love in this world is a predator. Love in this world wake you up at 3 am to argue with your spouse. Love in this world keeps lists and holds grudges. Love in this world starts arguments. Love in this world cannot let go of anger. Love in this world creates paranoia and is paranoid. Love in this world creates a state of confusion and clouds the truth and a persons ability to reason. Love in this world is willing to tear down and kill for all the wrong reasons. Love in this world is a prison keeper and holds others prisoner in their own home and mind. Love in this world is vengeful and spiteful and jealous. No one is ever good enough for love in this world and no one is ever good enough for the one that claims to love them in this world. Love in this world helps perpetuate your problems with no end to the problems in sight. Love in this world is abusive and strikes you. Love in this world can be murder because men have murdered those they claim to love. Love in this world makes you a hypocrite. Love in this world causes you to deceive someone into loving you then abandon him or her when they need you the most. Love in this world is a lie. Love in this world causes mothers to put their babies into dumpsters after they are born. The list goes on and on but you do not need me to write it down because I know that somehow and in some way you have somehow lived out these things written here and could probably add to this list if you decided to add to it.

I have a friend that is having problems in her relationship and I then asked her the question, saying, "What makes you think that any thing you have with this man even remotely resembles real, true love as God intends it?"

Then I pointed out the passage that I wrote here in Corinthians and then after that I started describing her relationship with her man and started the dialog with the opening statement, "Love is stalking." She then understood what I was trying to say. Her relationship did not match up with the biblical definition of love and her relationship does not match up with how God wants us to treat each other but her relationship does match up with the things that I described in this list of love in this world.

This world that we live in is one step from hell in the spiritual realm and a life's journey from heaven. We are many steps and a long walk from heaven although we can get there from here.

MY FATHER AND I ARE ONE AND THE SAME . . . .

This statement has always perplexed me and recently a possible meaning or understanding has come to mind. I was praying and noticed a pattern of details in my life that has to do with each time God has spoken to me. I noticed that whenever I made a choice and asked God what was going to happen, the outcome was shown to me in living pictorial memories that were sent to me in dreams. God was allowing me to see my future through dreams and these images that were sent to me were memories that were taken out of my mind at one point in time and placed into my mind at a previous point in time when I asked the question what is going to happen. Some images took 5 years to happen and other images took weeks or days to be seen. Then I noticed something very profound. All the choices that I am making on my own are leading me into circles and I go know where. Then I asked the being that is showing me these images how do I get off this path of repeated choice and repeated outcome. I need to follow the being that can see these things and lead me away. Then I asked another question and found the answer very disturbing. Who are you? Who are you showing me these things? The being that is shoeing me these things is ME. I am the one showing me these things. This being that I had mistaken for God is simply a very complete perfect version of me that exists outside of time and space and the physical body. There is no better guide than you leading you as long as you know where to go.

Now how can I explain this in a way that makes sense to someone that does not experience this? Imagine that you can go back and forth through time and space and can go and see yourself in the past when you were less educated and less sophisticated than you are now. Would you help yourself? Would you try and influence yourself into a life of higher learning and knowledge and reasoning? Would you talk to yourself as a child and try to help the child that was you learn something about yourself that could help?

I know that there is already a complete version of me that exists in heaven. This aspect or version of me has been systematically trying to help me and get some real knowledge about me into this thick head of mine. This version of me is trying to show me the error of my ways and teach me something new with a higher purpose and reasoning and outcome. I will write more about this latter if something comes to mind. All I can say now is that literally, A complete and whole and holy version of me and my identity that has nothing to do with the physical name that I have in this physical form is trying to get some real profound unshakeable knowledge of our existence and life into my brain. I look forward to really learning something and I look forward to the growth of myself into a higher form of me.

Come to God as a child . . . .

Many of the things that Jesus said perplex me. Why does Jesus say that we must seek him as a child and be as children? Lets give this a literal examination and see what comes to light.

First we must define the differences between children at the age of 2 to 3 and adults from the age of 35 to 80.

What can adults do that children at the age of 2 to 3 cannot do? Adults can drive, adults can comprehend complex mathematical equations. Adults can perform complex motor functions like repairing and building. Adults can do all sorts of amazing things that children cannot accept one thing and this one thing makes children superior to full-grown adults.

Children do things in the spirit and in their heart that adults do not do. Children love without condition of circumstances or race or age or religion or prejudice of any kind. Children laugh uncontrollably. Children are naturally joyous and explode with joy. Children are kind to strangers. Children accept people exactly as they are and are not condemning in any way. Infants trust and love and are dependant on those they gaze at from their crib and can do nothing else.

If children share any aspects of hatred or evil it is because they have been exposed to it and have been in this environment of hatred and are taught it from the ones that gave them birth.

Adults must relearn how to not judge people. Adults must relearn how to do the things that are listed here that children can do and adults cannot do. Look closely at children, not to discipline them but to see what they can teach you about God and yourself. What can they do that you cannot? Sometimes it is as simple as a smile. Children can smile more often than adults. Children are quick to smile and laugh and play and seek fun and happiness. Adults dwell on their doom and gloom and depression and how their life is so far gone and they have no hope. Children are alive with hope within them. It is easy to see if you look. Learn something from them. Let them teach you something for a change. My child has taught me more about God than I can ever teach him about God.

CHAPTER 16

OTHER ANCIENT SCRIPTURES ...

From
The Sophia of Jesus Christ ...
"All who come into the world, **like a drop from the Light,**
are sent by him to the world of Almighty, that
they might be guarded by him . . . ."

I have been studying other ancient scriptures and I want to give people a bit of advice. Before I offer advice or "exhort", they do a lot of exhorting in the bible, I had to look the definition up; I want to ask a question that you might want to ask for yourself. Why are there only 4 gospels and 12 apostles and many disciples? Each disciple and each apostle in the book of acts should have their own Gospel and their own book of Acts that is concerning and giving testimony to the things that they have seen and witnessed God do in the world around them.

These ancient scriptures are called the Nag Hammadi texts or the Nag Hammadi library. I am also reading other texts that are found under the title search on the Internet of "early Christian writings". My advice is simply this, do not discount these texts and do not cast prejudice and do not throw any preplanned disposition at these texts. Just read them if you are interested. These texts have some very strong grains of truth to them and there are things in these texts that they write about that can only come from being exposed to the presence of God and interacting with God. I have had things happen to me recently in my life and some of the things that I have seen and witnessed God do in my life are described through out the Nag Hammadi texts and the early Christian writings. These things are not described in the Bible.

I will give you one example of some things that I have found in the Nag Hammadi library than I have experienced first hand and have also been exposed to this type of phenomenon.

First I will tell you what happened to me. What I am about to describe to you happened to me before I died and happened to me before my wife came and took away my son and left me. My son was still with me and I had just finished watching the Passion. I never saw this movie in the theaters, I deliberately avoided these kinds of movies for reasons of things that I have described in this book, being crucified myself; I avoided seeing this movie. I had watched the movie and was sitting there contemplating and talking to God quietly in my mind and heart and asked the simple question that we all ask, "How did Jesus feel at that moment of his life and how did he feel toward mankind and the people that were hurting him during his crucifixion." This is the answer that I received. God spoke to me the next day before church and said," Look at your son, not from the outside in but from the inside out and you will see that when you spank your son or when you love your son his heart does not change, your son still loves you. As your son is there in front of you crying from being physically spanked (but not abused), or disciplined (you can get tears without spanking) he is still loving you in his heart and he is looking at you through crying eyes with a pain in his bottom and pure unwavering love in his heart. This is how Jesus sees us all the time, through eyes of pure love most of us will never know about. If you hurt Jesus or hate Jesus or love Jesus or do not love Jesus, the Heart of Jesus remains the same, a heart of pure love that is not changing. Jesus looked at those that crucified him with eyes of love even when they beat him and killed him."

When I began to contemplate this, ideas began to swirl in my mind. Scriptures came to mind, such scriptures like "come to God as a child . . ." and other things as well. Then I realized that my son that was not even 3 years old yet brought me closer to God, simply through observing his behavior, not by trying to teach him my own behavior. Children love and are love. This is the purity that we loose from birth to manhood and old age. Children love without condition. This is the AGAPE we need to give each other. Even when you beat or hurt them they still love. There are countless cases of abused children all over the country that will stand up and defend their abusive parents for reasons of love. As I contemplated this and pondered the concept that came into mind I walked into church expecting nothing and no supernatural event but something was about to happen to me. I was standing in the back and a power from God fell on me. **I can only describe it as light-water.** It was light and it acted like solid water, being viscous and flowing exactly the way water flows when you spill it or pour it or puddle it. The best way that I can describe what hit me was light-water. This light-water made me fall to my knees in the back of the church. People in the church describe it as being slain in the spirit but it was much more. This light-water fell on me and it gave me something that I can only describe as omni-awareness and it gave me a brief oneness with God. This power fell on me and it crippled me. I can also describe it as a drop of pure spiritual blood from the living God fell on me.

Now I have never read anything in the scriptures of the 4 gospels that mention anything of light—water or even use the words light-water as a descriptuon of anything **BUT** in the Apocryphon of John in the Nag Hammadi library they talk about it a lot. They mention the light-water in this book. I will also mention a few other things since I am writing about this aspect of what has happened to me. There are dozens of circumstances and situations and supernatural miracles that I have been able to experience but since we all have not experienced the same thing at the same time there is no common point of reference for me to share the experiences with you. What I am saying to you is that it is very difficult for me to talk about death with people that have not died yet because they have not died and we share no common frame of reference. It is easy to talk about my death to other people that have died because we have a shared experience in common so we can relate to each other. This is my dilemma. In the Pistis Sophia they talk about the light-power of Jesus. This I also witnessed. There are also passages in this book, which describe God as I have drawn him in my sketches and art.

These people that wrote these books were exposed to the mysteries of God. I am convinced of this. In the Pistis Sophia in the Nag hammadi library they also describe the HELPERS or the smaller orbs of light, which follow Jesus and do Gods will. The closest character in the bible that describes this being is the cherub. Other people that have died and been sent back have also seen the orbs of light and describe them as "helpers" I have heard this discussed in the NDE videos. The Helpers are also described in the Pistis Sophia as the (Parastatai). These people that wrote these ancient texts were exposed to the same mystery of God that exists to this day and have the same dilemma that I have, describing that which couldn't be described, it can only be witnessed.

If you are hungry for knowledge read and search (another word for pray) and have an open mind. What you are looking for will jump out at you and grab you, and then you will grab hold of those words and learn something. Evil hates it when you gain a scrap of knowledge that cannot be taken away from you again. There is more truth about God than can ever be written in the tiny 4 gospels of the Bible. Do not get me wrong, the bible and the 4 gospels are accurate also, there is just a great deal of knowledge that is missing.

CHAPTER 17

MY LIFE REVIEW ...

What can I say about my life review? I am still in awe as to how it has been given to me. The Life Review can also be considered to be judgment day referred to in the bible although I think that people at large, the NDE community and people that have not crossed over and returned have not made the correlation. If you do not know what a life review is and what I am referring to then you need to go find some life and death videos and listen to how those people explain the event because each person in the video has something in common that should be very startling when the evidence is aligned. People that never knew each other, people that live on opposite sides of the world and people that live in opposite sides of faith all describe the life review in exactly the same circumstances. They are given their life history in full view of them from beginning to end and shown themselves from the perspective of the other people that they encountered and saw themselves through the eyes of other people, all other people that they encountered to the very last day of their life. This concept can be made much more clearly in the videos because they can use visual aids to get the point across. Here is something that I might like to add, during the life review we become ourselves and then we become other people. We speak to someone else, and then we become the person that the words are spoken to and then while we are that person we can see how the other person interpreted us. Here in this trinity of communication we find the fault and the core of problems with humanity. People misunderstand each other. We do not understand what we are saying or how it will be received by the other person and we do not understand what is being said to us by the other person, so communication is lost and breaks down from almost the beginning of speech. I really do not expect a person that has not died and come back to understand this but I do know that people that have gone through their life review will find this very interesting and ponder this.

We try to get our point across but because of what we are in this state of being, the sinner or the" lack of knowledge" state of being, we don't know how to talk to someone and then we also find that we do not know how to listen to someone. Emotions are always in the way. If we could truly talk and truly listen then a lot of problems in relationships would cease to exist. How often have you apologized because one day you finally realized that you did not understand what the other person was saying and then while under that misunderstanding of what the other person said you did something or said something hurtful. Then later after examination you realized that you were wrong and did not understand what that person was saying and went to them and apologized.

My life review . . . a supernatural event that still continues . . .

As I have said earlier in this book. My life review is being done to me here and now. Other people die and get their life review but for some reason I am going through this experience while still in my body. I have had dreams and premonitions and visions and things of this nature all my life and at last it has finally dawned on me where this jumbled and fragmented information is coming from, it is coming from me. We are caught out of time and space during a life review. Right now as you are walking through your life and living it from the perspective of the first time event in your life, you are also dead and at the end of your life, reviewing it and seeing yourself and all the people in your life. When you are dead and in a life review, God is not showing you pictures of your life, he is showing you the real thing as it actually happened and happens and is happening. This is why God is referred to as the God of the past/ present/ future if you pay attention to how they refer to God at church sometimes.

So lets put this in terms of talking about you. The version of you that is in the future is giving or sending information to the version of you that is now, trapped in time and space and here on earth with the hope of giving you some type of information advantage over the adverse situation that you are in. In essence you are receiving telepathic signals from yourself, that is The You in the future and dead or outside this life and reality. You are getting show your life in the future, with images of things to come and also shown insight into other people, this is what people might interpret as mind reading or knowing something about someone that you could not possibly have known.

The more I learn, the more I learn that Jesus knew so much more than we can imagine. He hinted about it all the time in the scriptures. My real question is how did Jesus get this knowledge? Did he die out in the desert when he was there for 40 days being tempted? There is no way to know for certain.

So how exactly have I been given my life review? Sometimes I am given me life review in very subtle ways and sometimes very abrupt ways. I ask God a question and I receive images and concepts and situations through dreams while I sleep. These dreams are not "dreams" as you know a dream but they are images and memories of my life being given to me in an earlier time. I also see visions and knowledge comes to me while I am awake. I never really understand what I am seeing but I do know that it is a vision of my future and not just my imagination. I also have come to understand that my future and everyone's future is dictated by the choices that we make. So when ever I would ask God what was going to happen to me he would show me the outcome of certain choices that I made. This is also in line with the life review although it is from the first person perspective instead of the third person viewing perspective. In essence I have been making the same choices and running around in circles. The question now is how do I get God to help me make choices that will allow different outcomes that are in obedience to Gods will for me? I keep praying about this but I have yet to get a quick immediate response. Which means that response to this question could take a considerable amount of my life to teach me. Great.

There are passages in the bible about people that dream dreams and see visions. The real question, once you figure out that these things are real, is where does this information that is being injected into my brain coming from and why? What does it help or solve? As I look back and remember all the dreams and visions that I had I also remember that I was never able to change or correct an outcome, so the choices that I made played out in real life exactly as I dreamt them. So am I not getting enough information in the visions or what? There are hundreds of people that are out there suffering right now and being tormented because they are going through visions and dreams and see their future and the future of other people but can't do anything to change to outcome.

I have learned that the change comes from choice. If I watch closely enough concerning the choices that I make I can see how history has a nasty way of repeating itself in my life. The question is will I remain vigilant enough and remain strong enough in force of will and faith in God to change my next series of choices to get a different outcome.

There are those that will read about what has happened to me and then there are those that will experience the same things that have happened to me. We will not share all the same experiences but we will share some of the same experiences together.

Characteristics of Visions . . .

A vision is about something that happens in the future. Looking into the past is a different type of vision.

I want to make a list of some of the characteristics of a vision or receiving information about you from a future version of yourself. Visions begin with asking questions to God about certain aspects of you. The information that is given to you can never be forced by you. It is given at a time of Gods choosing. The information that comes will come in random images that are jumbled and seem to make no sense as if someone was showing you a film or pictures as fast as they can and you get no chance to really memorize what you see. A vision only comes once. Then you must try and remember or piece together clues that you remember. A vision is always about a choice that you have already made and never about a spectrum of possible choices that can be made. God never tells you what the vision means, it is simply shown to you and you must figure it out for yourself. Some visions come while you are awake and some come while you sleep. Both feel abnormal. It feels as if information is being injected into your consciousness. Visions are your memories that are being taken from your life in the future and given to you in the past. That is why it seems so familiar to you when the vision you were given comes into present time and you walk through it. A vision is a warp of time and space by you. It is being in two places at once and trying to struggle for consciousness while being in both places.

So let me describe it as it actually happened to me. I will try to explain this as plainly as possible and dispense with any mystery or intrigue and just tell the story plainly as it happens. I will be telling you things that will seem strange. I will also need to make several references to time. You need to imagine 3 places in time. I will use 5 years as a reference point. I will use 5 years ago and 5 years in the future from that moment. As I walked through all these moments in time they all seemed like the present to me or I perceived them as present time. It is called the reality of right now. Time is a strange thing. Right now is someone's future and right now is someone past. This moment right now is 5000 years into the future for some people and this moment right now is also 5000 years in the past for some people.

So the real question is how can we ever really change things that are going to happen to us? Anyway, back to explaining the vision and how it worked this one time for me.

5 YEARS AGO, I asked God a question. I asked God how a certain situation in my life was going to turn out and how a relationship was going to end up and how everything was going to turn out?

I fell asleep and was given a dream. In this dream I saw images and events and people that I had never met before and feel completely in love with people in that dream and it was as if I had lived a lifetime of events in the time frame of one evenings sleep.

I woke up completely in love with strangers that I had never met and could still feel their presence and their spiritual fingerprint all over me. I felt as if I had met real living people in this dream.

I was very upset because I had specifically asked God about one person and I was shown a completely different set of people in this dream. I was in love with someone in my life at the time and was shown someone else that I was in love with while in this dream. It was very confusing to say the least.

I passed off the dream/vision, as just another strange dream that I had and thought it meant nothing.

5 YEARS INTO THE FUTURE FROM THAT POINT IN TIME, the dream began to come to life and I slowly started to meet these people. Then the vision came to a complete circle. I was lying awake and I could feel God taking all the memories of those few months and taking them out of my consciousness and sending them back through time into my body and memory at the 5 YEARS AGO POINT. I had been given the chance not only to experience a true vision but also got to see how the dynamics of the situation work. So I got to experience the vision and walk through the events and live them out and also go to see how the mechanics of a vision and how it is given to people work.

In these paragraphs I am not trying to describe the particulars of my vision and what I saw and what I did, I am trying to tell you the characteristics of how the mechanics of a vision works so that you may be able to recognize it when it comes to pass.

TAKE TODAY'S
MEMORIES AND SEND THEM TO YOUR PAST . . .

Imagine taking today's memories and putting them into the mind of you yesterday and giving you no guidance or supervision or instructions. That is essentially how it works. Can The You of yesterday really understand the memories that The You of today has and recognize the dangers and the pitfalls and keep from making the same mistake once?

THREE TYPES OF VISIONS ....

This vision, today's memories given to your past is one type of vision. I have noted three basic types of visions in life. There is the vision of your future and what will occur through the choices that you have made.

There is the vision of seeing how other people perceive you and how they feel when you speak or act. This vision is seeing you through the eyes of others. These visions cause you to repent from certain things and actions. You will be led to apologize for actions and things that you have done. In these types of visions God shows you how you shatter other peoples hearts instead of trying to justify your anger or hatred.

There is the vision of seeing yourself how God sees you and seeing yourself through the eyes of God almighty. These visions feel like chastisement from God. They are designed to teach you about yourself and get you to repent and do things that you would not do such as apologize for certain actions and go to people and say, "I'm sorry". These visions can also be described as becoming self-aware.

I have described the 3 types of visions that I have been experiencing. There may be others such as seeing disasters and other types of events. These are global and not personal. The visions that I describe here are personal and are characteristic of the personal relationship that you have with God. I hope that this information here might help in understanding what is happening to you because when a person receives a vision there is never a manual that comes with it and you never get told what it means.

I have yet to see one of the true powers of God and that is being shown how to alter one of these visions and get a different outcome other than what was shown to me. How do we change choices midstream and become self aware enough in a short amount of time to actually alter events in our life that have already come to pass. Remember that from a certain point of view this is your yesterday although it seems like right now to you and this is your tomorrow although it seems like right now. Perhaps what I speak of now will be taught to me later in my life and I will learn how to alter my own path and become self aware enough to understand that I did in fact alter my destiny through choice.

For those of you that have the coincidence of reading this book and having a vision of your future events and then you see these events happen in your life, I hope that something written here helps. What I write here will not help people that do not have visions but it may help those that do have visions. You need to understand a few basic things. First, you are not crazy. I say this because these types of events will drive you to the point of insanity. These events are real, although you do not understand what is happening, remember these events are real. Slow down in your life and really look at what you have seen in your vision. Take the time to write it down and try to figure out the mystery that is your life. I cant tell you what your personal vision means but I have tried to describe the parameters of the events as they happen.

This mental loop of information is not all that I have seen and heard about how God manipulates time and space.

I have heard stories of God sending real life people back into the time/space continuum to help avert disaster for those people involved. God has done this for me through a second party. God altered time and space itself and sent a woman back to earth to help a person that was going to one-day help me. This is an amazing story in itself and if God can and is doing these things then they are very well hidden within our society and not being made public knowledge.

The old woman's Ghost . . .

I was sitting with a friend of mine and I had asked her if she had seen or done anything supernatural in her life and she proceeded to tell me an amazing story of how her life was saved by a woman that had been dead for many years. My friend refuses to tell the world this story and chooses to keep it to herself so I will speak in terms of no identities revealed. This friend of mine that was saved by the woman that had been already dead for 10 years was to later be a strong influence and take place in helping save my life in several different ways.

My friend was very young, about he age of 12 and she was going through disastrous circumstances in her life to the point that she might be killed. She was walking through a neighborhood and a woman sitting on a front porch asked her to help clean her house. My friend that was 12 at the time, agreed to help the old woman and spent several days or even weeks helping this old woman clean her house. Then one day the old woman came in close to her heart and started talking to her about the personal tragedy that she was enduring at the age of 12 and the old woman told her that it was all going to end soon and she was going to be safe and the problems and pain that was being done to her was going to stop.

A few days later the young girl of 12 came back to the house of the old lady with her mother and was there to simply help as usual. They found that the house was abandoned and all the cleaning that she had done was gone and the place was back to the way it was when she first started cleaning. Then a different woman in a car drove by and asked who they were and they said that they were there to help the old woman that lives there clean the house.

The woman in the car was the old woman's daughter. She said that there was no old woman living there because the old woman that lived there had been dead for 10 years. When they went inside, my friend that was 12 at the time had identified the old woman that she had been speaking with by a photograph of her still hanging on the wall and the woman that was in the car said that this was her mother that has been dead for 10 years and she could not have been talking with this woman in the photograph because she is dead. My friend that was 12 insisted that this was the woman even though no one believed her.

The old woman's prediction came true and the torment that was in her life at that time came to a halt through some type of circumstance.

Now this is a very powerful story. If we look at an over view of the story and the ability to warp reality then the possibilities and the applications are very mind boggling and staggering. God did this for my friend at an early age and in tern my friend at a later date came into my life and had a very strong impact on me.

So the real question is what did God do exactly? God sent a woman that had been dead for 10 years back into this reality to intervene for the benefit of others. I think that there are hundreds of people out there with stories like this and all these people are also unwilling to come forth to talk about what had happened to them. We can't have God be revealed to us and keep God hidden at the same time.

The true meaning of the book of revelations or the book of apocalypse means that God in all his abilities and aspects are revealed to mankind and God becomes fully know to us and we become aware of God. When will people find the courage to come forth and be a true witness to God even in the most supernatural of circumstances? Our society needs to organize and begin some type of informational data base where people can go and report supernatural circumstances in their life without fear of being ostracized in the community. People also need a place to go to study all the things that God has done for others in a supernatural way. God explained nothing to me, God just acted. Within those actions you can see that I am being spoken to but God is also very frugal with words.

There are organizations emerging but they are still in their newest stages of being accepted and know about. I understand that some doctors refuse to accept the facts of life after the body ceases to exist and doctors will not accept the ramifications that are possible to this reality. If doctors accept what is happening to dead people that come back to life after a few days as gospel truth then the way we define this reality that we live in must be altered. The selfishness would soon be over if people started accepting that these events that are happening to people all over the world are real.

CHAPTER 18

MORE QUESTIONS
THAN ANSWERS ABOUT GOD . . .

Now that I have a few scraps of information it leaves me with more questions than answers about God. I also have some speculative insights as to why God and Jesus did this instead of doing this. Before I write my questions that only God can answer I must first make a few statements of fact that I have learned. These statements are fact to me and not faith so there is a big difference in what I know to be fact and what I believe or speculate to be real. Faith believes in something that is unknown or uncertain. Fact knows without faith.

Here are the Facts that I have discovered:

1. God exists and God is real. Jesus is real and is The Savior.
2. Angels exist and angels are real.
3. Supernatural events are taking place everyday and mankind is being herded or guided to a destiny that we are unaware of at present time.
4. People can read minds and see into their future and into the future of others as well as a myriad of other supernatural things like healings and so on . . .
5. Evil exists and Demons are real. Most of them seem to be simply misguided spirits that once were people on earth that refused to do Gods will for them.
6. Hell exists and Heaven exists. I have been allowed to see into both arenas of domain.

7. The Garments of light exist; many people of earth have seen them, from the time of Jesus until present time. See ACTS 10:30 and read the single line . . .
8. The only beings that **do not know** God as fact are the spirits or people that are on earth in a corporeal form. Every other being in Heaven or Hell recognizes God and Jesus and Holy Spirit.
9. We do not cease to exist after the flesh is dead.
10. People out of their body can see into this world but we cannot see them.

Patterns of action I have noticed in God . . .

1. People have always mistaken Jesus for the Devil. These actions and patterns are talked about in the Gospels. When the demon known as legion was cast out of the man and thrown into the swine and the swine went running away the owner of the pigs called Jesus some very demonic identities. However, the demon recognized Jesus as the Christ. Other people in the gospels also called Jesus "Satan" and Jesus replied with the parable that a kingdom divided against itself cannot stand. This statement and pattern falls inline with the statement that I just made in fact number 8. Through out the bible the presence of God has always been described as being a fear filled thing," and an angel appeared to the Shepard's in the field and they were sorely afraid", What does this say about the real living God? We are constantly surrounded by evil and the devil in the hearts of people and in ourselves and in the invisible world around us and yet we are not fearful of this type of evil. What does this say about us?
2. God has always been the one to destroy the city and not the Devil. The Devil tried to stop Jesus from going to the cross over and over again by tempting him in the desert and also through the apostles and all the people that surrounded him.
3. God led Jesus to the cross not the Devil. God shed his blood on the cross for us. That is why the Devil did not want it to happen.
4. God has always been the one to send the prophet or Angel into the city to rescue people and then destroy the city as the people being rescued left. This type of action has also been predicted in the great rapture that is destined to take place. God has always given people a chance to get out or away, for those that believe and listen to Gods word, before God came in as a creature of wrath.
5. The Devil seems to be never mentioned in the dealings with Moses and the Pharaoh always seemed to be the great antagonist. What does this say to you?

6. I have also noticed that whenever there is a real life event of an angel that intervenes or interacts with someone in his or her corporal state on earth the angel never really speaks or gets to close or involved. The angels lead and guide and point but never really divulge any concrete information. They show people things and leave it to the person to try and figure out what they are seeing. I noticed this in the case of the man that died in Nigeria named Daniel. Angels led him while he was gone from here, into the afterworld but they never really told him anything, they just let him see things and observe. The angel never really stated what was really going on. The angel also had a garment of light. I would enjoy seeing this garment of light for myself.

Why didn't God do this and this and this . . . .

Since my death and resurrection or return it has brought to mind all sorts of avenues of action that God did not take and things that Jesus could have done gut did not do. Here is a premise that I have been wondering. Why didn't Jesus just set up camp here in earth and remain known as Jesus and let him self be made known after his resurrection and stay out in the open?

Instead of ascending as the scriptures tell Jesus could have stayed and taken hold of this world in a way that has never been done before. We all understand the concept of strongholds of evil that exist in our hearts and in the world. Where are the strongholds of Heaven on earth?

Jesus could have stayed and made himself known to those that killed him and continued to battle evil and fight in the manner that only Jesus could fight and still continued to heal and preach and be known as the Christ to this very day. Why does God allow the interim of time between the first and second coming of the Christ? So much evil and so much pain could have been prevented if Jesus could have simply stayed. I ask these questions because I know that these things are completely possible for God.

Why do the angels intervene so infrequently and when it happens it seldom becomes public knowledge. If there are these beings of light with garments of light and this incredible light power why is it keeping itself hidden from the entirety of the planet. There needs to be a common experienced miracle of epic proportions that needs to take place. There needs to be a single miracle or presence of God or display of God so that all can experience it and know the same thing at the same time. It is not fair to all people for one person to experience the presence of God and others remain ignorant of this type of presence. We all need to feel what it means to be sorely afraid, as it is referred to in the bible. It is time for revelations of God. It is time for God to be revealed to mankind. It is time for us all to experience the same miracle at the same time so that we may all know there is something out there other than ourselves and something other than this existence that we create for ourselves.

Exerts from the Gospel of Phillip . . .

As I said earlier in this chapter there are more questions than answers in dealing with God. Unfortunately God is the only one that can answer these types of questions that are systematically inspired by God in the first place.

I thought that I would write down a question or two that is inspired and a singular attitude and point of view that is growing within me. I will write down the exert from the Gospel of Phillip and then try and explain the types of questions that come forth and also the observations that are growing in me.

The Gospel of Phillip . . .
An ass which turns a millstone did a hundred miles walking. When it was loosed, it found that it was still at the same place. There are men who make many journeys, but make no progress towards any destination. When evening came upon them, they saw neither city nor village, neither human artifact nor natural phenomenon, power nor angel. In vain have the wretches labored.

First I wish to say that this is a very astute observation and correct. Many people labor in vain and do not know it. Here are the questions. How can we know that we are laboring in vain unless God and Son and Spirit take the time to show us that we are laboring in vain?

Once a person realizes that they are in fact laboring in vain in many aspects and many things in their life how can they find the power and resources to change unless God give it to them?

There must also be someplace to go. When a person turns away from something they must have someplace to point themselves and some type of direction. Where is there for us to go if we repent from anything?

I have made a simple observation about the bible. In many cases it makes astute observations but offers no solutions or alternative choices once a person does in fact choose to whole-heartedly repent. To repent is good but where is there to go once a person repents. This is one of the greatest hurdles that must be overcome by the person repenting.

This statement above from the gospel of Phillip offers an observation but no alternative solution so the scripture is rendered powerless in our lives. Faith must one day act or have action.

I am still in a state of trying to figure out exactly what God expects me to do here. I know all these things now but I am still rendered inert upon this world and cannot make an effective change in my life or in anyone else's around me. So my quest must continue. Questions are valid. They come out of us naturally. Every question has an answer and every statement and every truth has a questioning heart somewhere searching for it.

So, here I am at the end of one thing and at the beginning of something else. I once asked a few friends at work while I was doing construction what they would do with their time if they stopped drinking and doing drugs and they did not have an answer for me. My response to that is that I do not have an answer for them either. It seems apparent to me that there is nowhere to go. When you repent of something you need to have something to turn to in your life and believing is not enough. There must be action with faith. If people came to me and said that they wanted to stop doing these things I would not know what to tell them. You cannot find your way into God, God must lead you to him. I am in the same position as the alcoholics and the drug addicts and the prostitutes although I chose not to do these things and not to participate in certain things. It is as if I am now with Moses wandering in the desert. The world seems engineered for failure not success. The world is engineered for failure more than it is engineered for an individual to succeed.

Why has God always been so shrouded and secretive? Why does a God need to hide itself from man, its own creation and that which is under Gods dominion? Why has God always selected a few to be placed here and those few are always eaten alive and torn apart by the general masses?

Why does God refuse to give us all one single common denominator miracle that we can all see at once and all discuss at once and all figure out and understand and we can all be on the same page at the same time or to put a finer point on it, our education levels can all be evened out and we all know the same thing at the same time. As far as I know throughout biblical history there has never been a singular miracle that the entire population has witnessed.

I ask these questions because as a witness to God I know things and these are the natural questions that come about after meeting the living God.

From the pages of THE ACTS of the Apostles 1:6-9

"Lord, is it at this time You are restoring the kingdom to Israel?"

He said to them, "It is not for you to know times or epochs which the father has fixed by his own authority; but you shall receive power when the Holy Spirit has come upon you; and you shall be my witness (So . . . Does this mean that I am to do something that allows others to see God or am I the one that is going to see God perform something?**) both in Jerusalem and in all Judea an Samaria and even to the remotest part of the earth."**

God why are you hiding yourself from mankind? I can clearly see that this is happening, God is hiding himself from mankind. Why is our education of you being systematically dumbfounded as if we are being set up for failure and not success? I can ask this also because I can see certain patterns of events that are set in motion in our lives. If God chooses to hide himself then there must be a certain type of value or certain need that is created in our lives as spirits that needs to take place without the interference or interaction with the living God. It is as if God is watching and waiting to see what we will do with our choices. The more I learn about God and what God is and does the less I know and the less I understand. I will say this; if you seek God and Jesus expect to be seeking for a very long time. The deeper you get into the Heart of God the deeper it gets. God's heart is a bottomless pit of pure love and has no end to it.

When will God do what I speak of here? When will God give us all the same miracle at the same time? The only miracle that is foretold that fits this description is the second coming in the book of revelations. When will God even out our education about God and our knowledge of God and bring us all to the same place of awareness of God at the same time? This is what the world needs to help end all the lies and deceptions and illusions that we create in front of each other and we create in front of ourselves toward God. When will God show himself to all of us?

THE END OR A NEW
BEGINNING...
IF GOD WILL NOT
LET ME DIE HERE
PERHAPS I WILL
SEEK MY DEATH IN
JERUSALEM WITH
ALL THE OTHER
PROPHETS.